Waterfall Hikes of North Georgia

Waterfall Hikes of North Georgia

Jim Parham

milestone
press

almond, nc

Milestone Press, P.O. Box 158, Almond, NC 28702
www.milestonepress.com

book design by Denise Gibson/Design Den www.designden.com
& Jim Parham

Cover photographs by Jim Parham (front) & Mary Ellen Hammond (back).
All interior photographs are by the author unless otherwise indicated.

Library of Congress Cataloging-in-Publication Data
Parham, Jim.
　　Waterfall hikes of North Georgia / Jim Parham.
　　　　p. cm.
　　Includes index.
　　Summary: "Lists sixty day hikes to over 200 waterfalls on public lands
in the mountains of north Georgia. Each hike entry includes driving and
hiking directions, map and elevation profile, distance, and estimated hiking time, with a photograph of each waterfall"—Provided by publisher.
　　ISBN 978-1-889596-22-8 (alk. paper)
　　1. Hiking—Georgia—Guidebooks. 2. Waterfalls—Georgia—
Guidebooks. 3. Georgia—Guidebooks. I. Title.
　　GV199.42.G462P37 2011
　　917.5804'44—dc22
　　　　　　　　2010053618

Printed in the United States on recycled paper.

HIGH SHOALS FALLS
HIGH SHOALS SCENIC AREA

Table of Contents

Northwest Corner

Cohutta Mountains

Table of Contents (cont.)

Western Blue Ridge

Eastern Blue Ridge

Northeast Corner

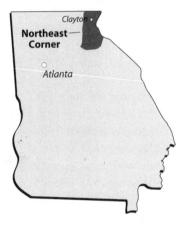

Appendices

Introduction

I've always believed that if you're going on a hike, it's a lot more fun and a lot more interesting if you have an exciting destination in mind. This could be a good view off the top of a rocky cliff, a section of old growth forest, or something more obscure, like a hillside known for wildflowers. Nothing captures my interest more, though, than a waterfall. There's something about hiking along with the sounds of crashing water all around that lifts my spirits and gets my blood pumping. I know that at any moment, around a sudden bend in the trail or as I step up to an overlook, I'll see before me all this water splashing down in a great froth of white. I have one thought, and it's always the same—"amazing!"

North Georgia marks the southern terminus of the Appalachian Mountains, a chain that stretches all the way to Maine. In Georgia the mountains span the top of the state from Chatsworth in the west to the South Carolina line east of Clayton, reaching altitudes nearing 4,800 feet. Even farther to the west, up in the corner below Chattanooga, is the tail end of the Cumberland Plateau, a flat-topped mountain that reaches north to Kentucky. The plentiful creeks, streams, and rivers here make lots of waterfalls.

Just how many waterfalls there are in north Georgia would be hard to guess. This book alone lists 200, all on public lands within reach of hiking trails. Head into the mountains, find a creek and start walking upstream, and at some point you'll find a waterfall. With thousands of creeks and rivers to choose from, it's not a stretch to say there must be thousands of waterfalls here. I'm sure humans will never see all of them, but this book will give you a healthy start.

First and foremost, this book is a hiking guide. Hikes listed here range from an easy half-mile walk that takes less than an hour to a strenuous twelve-miler that will take you most of a day. Novices and serious day hikers alike should be able to find something to suit them. On some of these hikes you'll walk out to one waterfall and then return to the trailhead. But I've always thought that if seeing one waterfall on a hike is good, seeing two, three, five, or eight is even better. So, on all of these hikes you can expect to at least see one waterfall, and sometimes many.

The vast majority of the hikes follow clearly marked, designated foot trails that make the routes easy to find. On most of them, the waterfalls are right on the trail or just off of it. Other hikes make use of trails created by the repeated footfalls of hikers who were interested in seeing a waterfall not on the main path. In this book, this kind of trail is sometimes referred to as a "goatpath." Such trails, while not marked, are also relatively easy to find and follow. A small few of the hikes require you to step off the trail and into the woods where there is no trail at all. Here you'll have to use any route-finding abilities you have to locate the waterfall up ahead. If you're up for it, it can be fun—and whether you find the waterfall or not, you'll still have a great hike.

People often want to know the best time to go on a waterfall hike. Any time is a good time to go on a hike, and it's also true that waterfalls change with the seasons. In north Georgia, winter is generally mild and wet. Spring is pleasant and sometimes wet. Summer is hot and can be dry or wet. Fall is usually pleasant and dry, unless a hurricane sends a lot of moisture off the Gulf, and then for a week or so it, too, can be wet—which is critical for optimum waterflows at the waterfalls. Consider all this before heading out on a hike, and you won't be disappointed. Generally speaking, though, if it has been a hot, dry summer, expect the smaller streams—especially those in the northwest corner—to be reduced to a trickle or dried up altogether. The larger streams, however, will still put on a pretty good show. After a few soaking rains or a prolonged wet season, you can expect everything to be at its best. What about the dead of winter? There's not much that's prettier than a waterfall covered in ice.

So—flip through the book and pick a hike that looks interesting. Then head for the mountains and out onto a trail. Before you know it, your spirits will lift, and you'll get that "full-body energy rush" feeling that comes only from standing in the presence of a pounding, splashing waterfall.

Hiking Guidelines

Gear Checklist

Nothing can ruin a good hike quicker than leaving something essential behind. Remember the scout motto? Be prepared. Here's a checklist of items for a day hike.

Footwear
- comfortable hiking boots or shoes you don't mind getting wet
- woolen or synthetic socks that fit well (no cotton)

Outerwear (be prepared to add layers; no cotton shirts or jeans)
- shorts or light pants and quick-dry t-shirt (this is your base layer)
- cap or wide-brimmed hat

In Your Daypack
- lunch/high-energy snacks
- water (2 liters per person)
- insect repellent
- personal first-aid kit
- sunscreen and lip balm
- rain jacket (always)
- long-sleeved shirt (always)
- emergency flashlight
- map and/or guidebook
- small plastic trash bag

Nice To Have
- walking stick or hiking poles
- pocket knife or multi tool
- camera

Clothing & Fitness

Dress for the weather. The key word to remember is layers. The weather in the north Georgia mountains can be very fickle. A day that starts out with abundant sunshine and warm temperatures can quickly turn to a cold fog or a sudden thunderstorm. No matter what the forecast, be prepared with multiple layers. A rain jacket over a long-sleeved shirt over a short-sleeved shirt and a hat to top it off will keep you warm in most conditions. If you're hot, take it off. If you're cold, put it on. And remember, leave your cotton at home.

Get used to walking in wet shoes. Of the 60 hikes listed in this book, at least half require crossing a stream once, twice, or many times. It just goes with hiking to waterfalls. Some people like to stop, take off their shoes to cross a creek, and then put them back on. After the third or fourth crossing this gets pretty tedious and begins to seriously cut into your hike time. Not only that, crossing a stream barefoot on slippery rocks is asking for trouble. Choose supportive footwear that you don't mind getting wet (it doesn't hurt your shoes) and will let the water drain out in a reasonable amount of time. Then just splash on through and be on your way.

Assess your fitness level. All the hikes in this book can be accomplished in a day or less, sometimes much less. The approximate hiking time listed for every hike assumes an average level of hiking fitness. Attemping an all-day hike "right off the couch" is not recommended. Before heading into the woods, assess your fitness level and choose a hike that matches what you honestly think you can accomplish in the time you have available.

Safety

Getting to the Trailhead

For many of the hikes in this book, getting to the trailhead is no big deal. All of Georgia's state parks and many of its recreation areas where popular waterfalls are located have well-maintained paved roads and parking lots. However, there are also quite a few trailheads that can be reached only by traveling on unimproved roads. Driving a vehicle on a winding, rocky, steep mountain road is significantly different from traveling on smooth asphalt. Even if you are accustomed to gravel roads, it's a good idea to take things slowly and be extra careful. Here are some driving tips to ensure a safe and enjoyable experience.

- First of all, slow down—*really* slow down. A vehicle does not respond the same way on loose stones and dirt as it does on a paved surface. Too much speed and you'll drift dangerously to the outside of curves, where safe braking becomes impossible. Remember, the idea is to enjoy the scenery, not make time.
- While driving, keep your eyes on the road. If you want to look at a view, stop the car in the middle of the road if you need to (as long as you're not on a blind curve) and take a look. Chances are no one is behind you, and you can move on or pull over if another vehicle comes along.
- Without constant grading, even the slightest uphill will eventually develop a washboard of corrugated bumps. You're most likely to encounter them on the inside of uphill curves, but they can crop up almost anywhere. Hit these with any speed at all, and they can bounce you right off the road—not to mention rattling your car and your teeth.

- Approach blind curves with caution. Some forest roads are single lanes with turnouts for passing. On a curve, keep to your side of the road and take it slow. You could meet an oncoming vehicle—and it may be a big logging truck taking up the entire road.
- Use extra caution at stream fords. Getting to some of the trailheads in this book requires that you ford a stream one or more times. Before crossing, take a good look at what you'll be driving through. Does your vehicle have enough clearance that the undercarriage won't drag in the water? Is one side of the ford shallower than the other? Are there any obstacles in the water? Once you start across, take it slow. If the stream is in flood, don't try to cross it. This *is* Georgia, but it's not the place to play Dukes of Hazard. On the other side, be sure to pump your brakes a few times while you're rolling to dry them out.
- Avoid these roads altogether during inclement weather. Winter snows can turn a mountain road into a toboggan course, and day after day of heavy rains or freezing and thawing temperatures can turn a hard-packed surface into mush.
- Always fill your gas tank before heading out.

On the Trail

Safety on the trail is as much about using good common sense as it is about anything else. Basically it boils down to so many do's and don't's, plus things to look out for. Here's a short list.

- Do let someone know your plans for the day before you go.
- Don't hike alone.
- Do dress appropriately and pack the items listed on p. 12.
- Don't start a long hike late in the day.
- Do keep your shoes on while crossing a creek or river.
- Don't cross a waterway in flood.
- Do carry plenty of drinking water.
- Don't drink water straight from the creek.

Things To Look Out For

- **Bears** Bears seem to be the number one thing people are afraid of encountering on a hike. In reality, the chances of meeting a bear on the trail are slim. When you do, the bear usually high-tails it for the nearest laurel thicket. Should you meet up with an aggressive bear, stand your ground. These animals can run much faster than you and they can climb trees. Make yourself look and sound as big as possible—wave your arms, shout, bang on something loud. This usually is enough to scare a bear away.

- **Snakes** Snakes are the second most feared thing in the woods. The chances of seeing a snake are good if you spend enough time outside. In the north Georgia mountains there are two types of venomous snakes to be concerned about—copperheads and rattlers (timber, pigmy, and eastern diamondback). Here again, use common sense. If you see or hear a snake in the trail, stop, assess the situation, and wait for the snake to move on or choose an alternate path around it.

TIMBER RATTLER You can recognize a venomous snake by its triangular shaped head.

- **Stinging Insects** There's nothing worse than bumping into a nest of angry hornets or disturbing a colony of yellow jackets or ground wasps. Such an encounter can quickly turn a peaceful walk in the mountains into a complete panic, with people running pell mell through the woods screaming and tearing their clothes off. Those stings can hurt like the dickens, and for anyone who is severely allergic they can be deadly. If you have such an allergy, never hike without your epi-pen. And everyone should always be on the lookout; hornets like to build their gray, football-shaped nests over water, so be especially careful around creeks and streams.

- **Poison Ivy** Of all the plants in the mountains, this one seems to be the most prolific. It grows just about everywhere, but it

HORNETS NEST They're gray, and shaped like a large football.

loves moist woodlands and areas around moving water. Since many a waterfall in north Georgia is guarded by the stuff, it's a plant you'll want to learn to recognize. Basically it grows in two ways—as a vine that climbs trees, and as individual plants living in vast colonies on the ground. Wading into a patch or grabbing hold of a hairy vine poses no immediate threat, but wait about 24 hours and if you're allergic (as many people are), you'll develop a rash of intensely itchy red blisters wherever the plant touched your skin. If you've had more exposure than that, be prepared to suffer. The rash can take weeks to dry up and go away, and often progresses to an oozy mess before it's gone. Should you inadvertently make contact, wash thoroughly with cold water in the nearest stream and hope for the best. You can also purchase over the counter preparations, though these must be applied soon after contact.

POISON IVY Look for the distinctive three-leaf pattern or hairy vines.

Crossing Streams

CROSSING A STREAM THE SMART WAY.
Clasp arms and work as a team.

If you plan on seeing many waterfalls, you'll have to cross a creek or a river at some point. Sometimes you'll get lucky and the trail will be developed enough to have bridges. Most times, though, you'll have to get your feet wet. It's not too difficult to keep the rest of your body dry if you just remember to use a few simple techniques.

When you approach a stream crossing, size it up. Is it small enough to hop across? Are there stepping-stones and do they appear to be stable? How deep is the water? Can you move upstream or downstream to find a better place to cross?

If you can hop across or use stepping stones, by all means do. And if you don't already use a walking stick, look around you for a temporary one. Having three points of contact with the bottom makes you many times more stable. Beware of crossing on logs. Sometimes they make for a good bridge, but often they will roll with you or break halfway across. Finally, if the water is more than ankle deep and/or 10 feet or more across, and especially if the bottom looks slippery, unclip the waist strap on your pack (you want to be able to ditch it in an instant so it won't drag you downstream should you fall in), clasp your hiking partner(s) by the arms, form a circle, and everyone walk across together. You'll be surprised at how you can negotiate across strong current, over slick rocks, through deep water using this method.

At the Waterfall

Every year people die because of something stupid they did at a waterfall. People have died at some of the waterfalls listed in this book. Here's what usually happens. They try to climb up the cliff or steep slope beside a waterfall to get a better view or take a picture or make an attempt to reach the top, and then they slip and fall. They try to peer over the edge at the top, and then they slip and fall. They try to climb the waterfall itself, and then they slip and fall. Everything near a waterfall—rocks, roots, fallen trees—is wet and slippery. If you do any of these things, it's only a matter of time before you slip

THIS WARNING SIGN SAYS IT ALL.

and fall, too. At best you'll twist an ankle or break an arm, and it could be fatal. Certainly your stupid mistake will ruin what could have been a nice hike for you and everyone else. *Always exercise extreme caution and common sense around waterfalls.*

Hunting Season

During the fall and on select dates during the spring, if you're hiking in the national forest there's a chance you'll run into game hunters. Most of the time, especially during small game season, this is not a problem. However, on opening day of rifle deer hunting season, around major holidays, and during special "quota hunts," it *can* be a big deal. On these days, in some places, it can seem that the woods are full of hunters—and you might not be comfortable with that. Regardless of whether you are or not, it's a good idea to wear bright colors in the woods during huntung seasons. For specific hunting dates, check the website at www.gohuntgeorgia.com or call one of the wildlife contacts in Appendix A. Hunting is not allowed in Georgia State Parks, so contact that office (also in Appendix A) if you want to be sure you won't be sharing the woods with hunters.

Waterfall Information

In his 2006 guidebook, *Waterfall Hikes of Upstate South Carolina*, author Thomas E. King provides such a complete and thoughtful description of waterfalls—including what defines them and guidelines for classifying, rating, and measuring them—that it seems pointless to attempt to devise another one. I am therefore grateful to him for the use of four sections from his book, slightly adapted and reproduced here.

What Is A Waterfall?

A precise definition of a waterfall is difficult to find. Most dictionaries and encyclopedias refer to a waterfall as a more or less vertical stream of water that flows over the edge of a cliff that has eroded away. A waterfall is also sometimes defined as a cascade of water crossing rocks that have not yet eroded, producing what is commonly known as a rapid, although a cascade is a generic term for any flow of water. A small creek can be said to cascade downstream over rocks. A cascading flow of water can be any height, from a few inches to several hundred feet. Each section of a waterfall is sometimes referred to as a cascade.

Different sources set different minimum heights, ranging from 5 to 20 feet, for descending water to qualify as a waterfall. Other points to consider:

- Must water flow over the falls be constant?
- What is the minimum volume of water flow acceptable (e.g. cubic feet per second) to qualify as a waterfall?
- What is the minimum degree or angle at which the water must fall or flow downstream?
- What is the origin of the waterfall—a constantly flowing stream, a spring from beneath the earth, melting ice or snow?

This book uses the following criteria to define a waterfall:

- A waterfall is a complete unit, sometimes composed of two, three, or more segments. Two segments miles apart are considered two separate waterfalls.

- Segments (each with a significant drop) only 10 feet apart can qualify as a section (e.g., upper, middle, or lower) of the same waterfall. To qualify as a waterfall, one segment of the falls must be at least five feet high.
- Most generally accepted true waterfalls must be located on a river, creek, or stream that provides a source of water at least annually.
- Most waterfalls have a significant amount of water flowing over boulders or plunging down a cliff. However, some very low-volume waterfalls are attractive because of the shape of the rocks or the striations of color in the rocks over which the water flows. Such low-volume flows are called trickles.

One day a waterfall can be a gentle trickle of water gracefully gliding over bedrock. The very next day after a rainstorm, that same waterfall changes its nature and shouts out its presence with a thunderous rush of water.

Some people might say that the shoals, rapids, and low-flow trickles listed in this book are not waterfalls. However, based on observations and information in other guidebooks, every waterfall listed meets the requirement of water dropping five feet or more in elevation over a very short distance.

Waterfall Structure & Classification

Waterfalls are classified into the following categories according to the physical structure of the segments:

- **Block**
  A wide flow of water extending uninterrupted across a river or creek.
  (Example: Dicks Creek Falls, p. 24)
- **Cataract**
  Typically occurring on torrents (large rivers), with a high volume of water.
  (Example: Jacks River Falls, p. 58)

- Fan
  A falls that widens at its base.
  (Example: High Shoals Falls, p. 154)
- Horsetail
  Water falling in a vertical drop, then making contact with the
  rock surface behind the water, causing the water to spray out or
  change direction from the original path.
  (Example: Little Rock Creek Falls, p. 112)
- Plunge
  A fall of water that makes no contact with the rock surface behind
  it; also called a freefall.
  (Example: Lula Falls, p. 34)
- Rapids
  A turbulent flow of water, usually through rocks, often navigated
  by whitewater rafters and canoeists. Rapids are ranked as Class-
  es I through VI, in ascending order of difficulty. Rapids usually
  consist of less than a single five-foot drop.
  (Example: Edge of the World, p. 138)
- Segmented
  Parallel falls where several streams (or part of one stream) flow
  over the same ledge side by side (twin, triplet, etc).
  (Example: Upper Falls on Blood Mountain Creek, p. 182)
- Sluice (Chute)
  Water descending through a constricted passage.
  (Example: Upper Falls on Holcomb Creek, p. 216)
- Tiered
  Water flowing in multiple drops over several sections of the falls
  (double, triple, quadruple).
  (Example: Desoto Falls, p. 186)
- Waterslide
  Water gliding in a thin sheet over slick or mossy rock slabs.
  (Example: Bridal Veil Falls, p. 265)

Many waterfalls are combinations of the segments listed above.
For example, Upper Falls on Low Gap Creek (p. 162) starts with a
slide, then ends in a plunge.

Rating Waterfalls

Waterfalls in this book follow the rating system below:

- Nice

  These waterfalls are usually small (5-15 feet high) with a low volume or trickle of water. May appeal only to serious waterfall buffs.

- Fair

  Small waterfalls (10-30 feet) on smaller streams.

- Good

  Larger and higher falls (25-75 feet). Usually very photogenic.

- Excellent

  Very appealing (50-100 feet). Considered beautiful, very photogenic.

- Spectacular

  Impressive in size (100 feet and higher) and water flow. Ideal for viewing and photographing.

It's important to note that the pleasure afforded by a waterfall does not correspond to its rating. Rating a waterfall is very subjective. Even falls rated only fair may be very appealing, depending on the perception of the observer.

Measuring Waterfalls

Many criteria used for classifying waterfalls are subjective. For example, the height of a falls is measured from the uppermost precipice over which the water flows to the lowest point of contact in a pool or stream or over boulders. However, what constitutes the base of a falls is often a matter of opinion. Most reported heights of waterfalls are only estimates. Even if the height were measured with sophisticated devices, the actual top and bottom of the falls would have to be identified before measuring, and sometimes that is not possible.

How To Use this Book

Information for each hike is broken down into different categories.

- **Hike Name**
  The hike name is at the top left hand side of the opening spread. Often this is also the name of the trail you will hike on or the waterfall you will see.
- **Waterfall Photos**
  Directly below the hike name (and elsewhere in the entry) are photos of the waterfalls you'll see on your hike. Below the photo are the class, height, and rating of the waterfall at optimal flow.
- **Hike Data**
  Below the hike name you'll find the hike data.
  Distance is always total distance—how far you will walk from the time you leave the trailhead until you return to the trailhead.
  Type refers to the hike's route configuration. You might walk a loop, an out-and-back where you go to a certain point and then retrace your steps, a lollipop, T- or Y-shape, or some other variation.
  Number of Falls tells how many waterfalls you can expect to see on the hike.
  Dry Feet should be thought of as a question. Will you be able to do the entire hike with dry feet? "Yes" means you will keep your feet dry. "No" means your feet will definitely get wet. "Maybe" means you may be able to do the hike with dry feet, but chances are they will get wet.
  Start Elevation is the elevation in feet at the trailhead. Use this in conjunction with the map's elevation profile. If it's a high number like 3,800 feet, you'll likely start out at a high point and go downhill to get to the waterfalls. A low number means you'll probably start out walking uphill.
  Total Ascent is the cumulative elevation gain over the course of the hike. The higher the number, the more strenuous the hike.
  Land Manager refers to the public agency that oversees the trails you will be walking on. In this book the agencies listed are abbreviated

as follows: National Park Service (NPS), United States Forest Service (USFS), Georgia State Parks (State Park), and Georgia Department of Natural Resources (GA DNR).

Fee refers to whether or not you'll have to pay a use fee or parking fee. For example, $3 means per vehicle and $3 pp means per person.

- **Hike Description and General Information**
  Following the first photo and hike data is a general description of the hike and/or interesting information related to the hike or its location. This section is not meant for directional purposes.

- **Bonus Falls**
  Occasionally on the drive to the hike you will pass a waterfall not on the hike route. Each of these waterfalls is highlighted in a gray box with specific information on the falls and how to reach it.

- **Directions to the Trailhead**
  Specific driving directions to the trailhead are given, usually from the closest town. GPS coordinates for the trailhead are also provided.

- **Trailhead Locator Map**
  Located adjacent to the trailhead directions, this gives you a clear idea of where the trailhead is and shows the route given in the text.

- **Hiking Directions**
  These are turn-by-turn directions for the hike route. Use of a GPS is not a requirement for hiking, but the exact mileage is given for each turn or entry in the directions. This lets you know how far you've come and how far you still have to go to get to your destination. Hiking distance information was determined with a GPS receiver unit.

- **Route Map**
  The hike route map is always placed in the same spread as the hiking directions. All maps are to scale and show the hiking route, waterfall locations, and side trails you'll encounter. Mileposts from the written hiking directions are posted on the map where there are no obvious landmarks for reference. The elevation profile at the bottom of the map provides a basic idea of how much up and down walking to expect. Keep in mind that a short hike of under a mile, climbing 40 feet, descending 70 feet, and then climbing 30 feet may *look* more difficult than an eight-mile hike that gains 300 feet, descends 500 feet, and then climbs 200 feet. This is because every profile uses a different scale, determined by the elevation numbers along the side of the profile relative to the distance numbers along the bottom.

Northwest Corner

Falls on West Rim of Cloudland Canyon

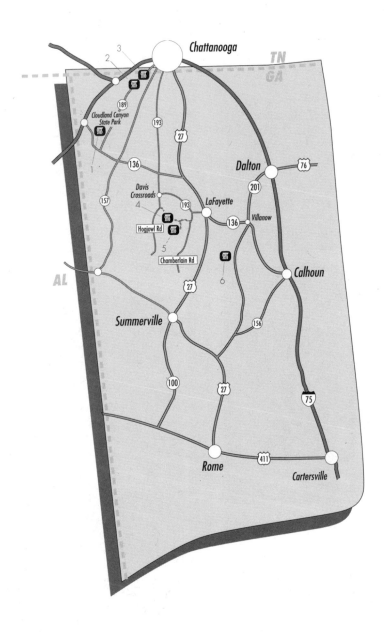

When it comes to waterfalls, northwest Georgia is one of the state's best-kept secrets. It's northeast Georgia that gets all the glory, which is just fine with the folks who live in the northwest corner. They like the peace and quiet that comes with fewer tourists, and they know what they have in their backyard. In fact, northwest Georgia not only has beautiful waterfalls, it has something equally important to hikers—excellent foot trails that lead to them.

From a geological point of view, these mountains are different from their eastern neighbors. Lookout Mountain and Pigeon Mountain, in the farthest northern corner, are actually plateaus—that is, they're relatively flat on top and rimmed with stone bluffs. Streams cut down through them, forming steep canyons, gorges, gulches, and "gulfs." Hikers looking to reach the waterfalls and pools at their bases must descend from the top the best way they can, by steep trail or wooden steps. The drawback is that what goes down must also go back up; you'll finish your hike going uphill.

Just to the east of the plateaus is the ridge and valley region. Here the mountains form long, uninterrupted ridges reaching generally from south to north. Small creeks that start on top drop quickly to join the larger streams below. Hikes here tend to start at the bottom, ascend steeply, and then meander along the ridgetops. On these trails you get to finish your hike going downhill. In the end, you can't go wrong with any trail you choose.

THIRD FALLS IN SITTONS GULCH

Sittons Gulch Trail

Hike Distance:	5.4 miles
Type of Hike:	Lollipop
Number of Falls:	5+
Hiking Time:	Half day
Dry Feet:	Yes
Start Elevation:	1,800 ft
Total Ascent:	1,476 ft
Land Manager:	State Park
Fee:	$3

FIRST FALLS
Class: Plunge   Height: 75 ft   Rating: Excellent

Sittons Gulch. It sounds like something from the Wild West days where some fellow named Sitton is waiting in a hideout to ambush you. Let's hope that's not the case, but you may feel a bit "bushed" after tackling—not once but twice—the steep staircase of over 600 steps that begins and ends this hike.

Cloudland Canyon State Park is Georgia's northwesternmost park, sitting atop Lookout Mountain, which forms the southernmost end of the greater Cumberland Plateau. Unlike the mountains to the east, Lookout Mountain is pretty much flat on top. On a plateau, streams erode the earth from the top downward, carving out canyons with sheer limestone walls. On this hike, you'll have to start at the rim and work your way down via steps between the cliffs. Plateau waterfalls tend to be high plunge falls, with huge deep pools at the bottom. This is certainly the case for most of the waterfalls you'll encounter on this hike.

Northwest Georgia summers tend to be hot and dry. As the season wears on, water levels in the streams typically drop. Keep this in mind when you hike. In late winter, spring, and early summer, and after heavy rains, the falls here will really rumble. Later in the year, smaller cascades might be reduced to a trickle.

The Sittons Gulch portion of this hike begins just below the second falls. Here you'll cross a high footbridge right over the top of the third falls. Now well into the canyon, the trail follows the gradient of Daniel Creek past numerous smaller falls, cascades, and rapids. Just beyond the fourth falls a small feeder stream enters from the left, and you'll notice a small cascade just above the trail. The casual hiker might just take a quick look and keep on going, but here's where it pays to

THIRD FALLS
Class: Plunge Height: 25 ft Rating: Good

explore a bit more. Take a rough scramble above and beside that first drop and you'll see that West Rim Falls, the highest falls in the park is just upstream. From the rim downward it forms a triple-tiered drop of 180 feet or more.

The remainder of the trail is a hiker's delight. Wildflowers abound in spring, hemlocks tower overhead, and the numerous rapids and small waterfalls will keep your senses occupied. If you're looking for a place to cool off, there's a great swimming hole near the far end of the hike.

SECOND FALLS
Class: Plunge Height: 100 ft Rating: Excellent

Sittons Gulch Trail (cont.)

Getting to the Trailhead

Cloudland Canyon State Park is located just west of the intersection of GA 136 and GA 189 atop Lookout Mountain, south of Chattanooga, TN.

GPS Coordinates
N 34° 50.01' W 85° 28.84'

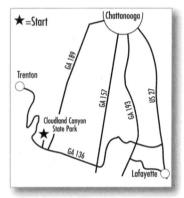

Hiking Directions

Begin From the day-use area, walk to the canyon rim and follow signs leading to the falls.

Mile 0.2 Bottom of first tier of steps. Turn right to the falls.

Mile 0.3 Many steps later, turn left to first falls.

Mile 0.5 First falls. Return to the last junction and follow the trail/steps to second falls.

Mile 0.8 Reach bottom of steps. Turn left to second falls.

Mile 0.9 Second falls. Return to the last junction and follow signs onto Sittons Gulch Trail.

Mile 1.0 Cross Sittons Creek on

WEST RIM FALLS
Class: Tiered Height: 180 ft Rating: Good

a high bridge. Third and fourth falls are just below.

Mile 1.2 Cross a low-flow stream. When water is present in this stream, you'll see West Rim Falls to your left. If you walk upstream a short distance, you'll see that the falls is very high (180 feet or so) and begins on the top of the western rim.

FOURTH FALLS
Class: Block Height: 12 ft Rating: Good

Mile 2.5 Between here and West Rim Falls you'll pass numerous small waterfalls and swimming holes on Sittons Gulch Creek. Turn left here to begin the end-loop lollipop portion of trail.

Mile 2.7 Turn right at trail junction. The trail coming in from the left here should have a wire strung across it.

Mile 2.9 Close the lollipop loop and return to the start the way you came down.

Mile 5.4 Finish.

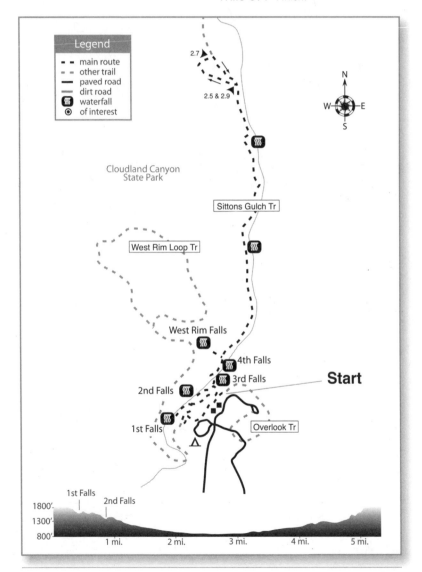

Lula Lake Land Trust Loop

Hike Distance:	4 miles
Type of Hike:	Loop
Number of Falls:	2
Hiking Time:	Half day
Dry Feet:	Maybe
Start Elevation:	1,362 ft
Total Ascent:	934 ft
Land Manager:	LLLT
Fee:	None

LULA FALLS
Class: Plunge Height: 100 ft Rating: Excellent

Two days. That's how many days each month you have the chance to hike to these waterfalls. Lula Falls and Lula Lake Falls are managed by Lula Lake Land Trust, a nonprofit organization dedicated to preserving the natural beauty of the Rock Creek watershed.

Just what is a land trust? It can be many things, but one of its purposes can be to ensure public access to private land. In 1994, local landowner Robert Davenport bequeathed his land around Lula Lake to form the trust. Since then LLLT has grown to protect over 4,000 acres of the Rock Creek watershed. Today it is used for everything from scout campouts to outdoor classrooms to an experimental forest. The first and fourth Saturdays of every month are known as "open gate" days, when the gates are open to the general public. Hikers, cyclists, and nature enthusiasts bump down the dirt road to the trailhead where they find over six miles of well-maintained trails and two magnificent waterfalls.

On this hike, in addition to viewing the falls you'll get the chance to walk through an experimental orchard of hybrid American chestnut.

These young trees planted by LLLT are not so tall now, but given time and a little bit of luck, they should grow to be giants like their ancestors of old.

A generation has passed since chestnut trees dominated our southern mountainsides. They once grew very tall with huge girths and provided lumber, firewood, nuts for food, and honey from their fragrant blooms. Early European settlers would have had difficulty imagining a forest without this mighty tree. But early in the 20th century an exotic fungal blight attacked the trees, and entire forests were wiped clean until only a few small chestnut trees survived. From this small reserve, the American Chestnut Foundation is diligently working to reintroduce a hybrid that will withstand the blight.

Hiking in Lula Lake Land Trust is a real treat. On this hike you'll first make your way down to the falls via North Creek Trail, which parallels Rock Creek. It's only a mile down to the first waterfall and just a little past that to the second. At this point you could just turn back, but there is so much more to enjoy here.

After seeing the first falls and then negotiating the spur trail to the second falls, you'll hike up and over the bluff on High Adventure Trail. This is a fitting trail name, as you'll find out. You'll get great views over the Rock Creek watershed and enjoy a stiff breeze when you top out to overlook the Chattanooga and Chickamauga Valleys—it's an awesome clifftop view. A stroll through the chestnut orchard continues into the woods and brings you back to the trailhead.

LULA LAKE FALLS
Class: Tiered Height: 30 ft Rating: Good

Lula Lake Land Trust Loop (cont.)

Getting to the Trailhead

From Chattanooga, take Ochs Highway from St. Elmo up Lookout Mountain for 3.3 miles. Turn left on Lula Lake Road and go 4.5 miles. Turn left at signs for Lula Lake Land Trust Open Gate Day. It is 0.8 mile from here to trailhead parking.

GPS Coordinates

N 34° 55.33' W 85° 22.85'

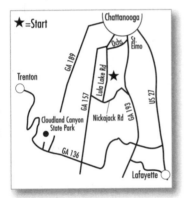

Hiking Directions

Begin Follow the exit road out of the trailhead parking area.

Mile 0.3 Turn right on Ford Road Trail, cross the creek, and then turn left after 100 yards onto North Creek Trail.

Mile 0.9 Turn left onto Connector Trail down to the bridge and then right on Old Railroad Grade Trail.

Mile 1.0 Reach Lula Lake. There's a picnic area here, and Lula Lake Falls—a 30-foot tiered drop—is at the head of the lake. After viewing the falls, continue down Old Railroad Grade Trail.

Mile 1.3 Overlook Lula Falls, 100 feet high. Just beyond is a spur trail leading to the base. The trail is very steep with loose rocks. After descending and coming back up again, continue on Old Railroad Grade Trail.

Mile 1.9 Just before the property boundary, turn right on High Adventure Trail and go up between the bluffs. This trail lives up to its name—you'll use an anchored rope to assist you as you ascend.

Mile 2.2 Junction with Bluff Road Trail. There's a great overlook with a picnic table here. Turn right on Middle Road Trail and walk down through the experimental chestnut orchard.

Mile 2.5 Bear left where Connector Trail turns right to Lula Lake.

Mile 2.8 Turn left on Turkey Trail.

Mile 3.0 Homestead Trail exits right. Stay on Turkey Trail.

Mile 3.3 Turn right on Ovenbird Trail.

Mile 3.6 Turn right on Middle Road Trail.

Mile 3.7 Homestead Trail enters from right. Stay on Middle Road.

Mile 3.8 Turn right on Middle Road Cutoff Trail.

Mile 3.9 Turn right, go down the hill, then turn left over the footbridge to the trailhead.

Mile 4.0 Finish.

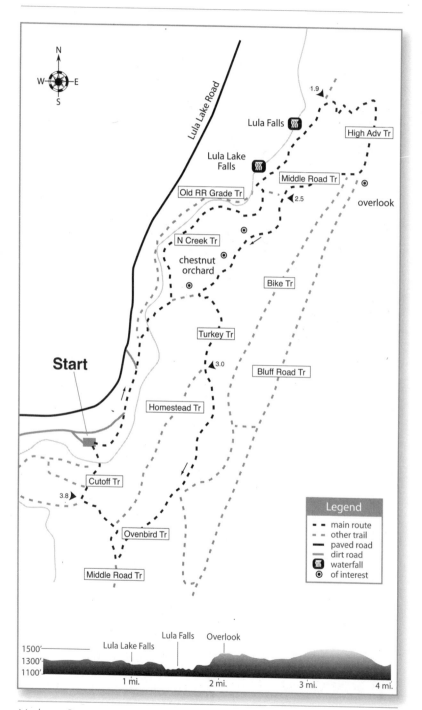

N
W E
S

Lula Lake Road

Lula Falls ♨

Lula Lake Falls ♨

High Adv Tr

▶1.9

Middle Road Tr

overlook ⊙

Old RR Grade Tr

▶2.5

N Creek Tr ⊙

chestnut orchard ⊙

Bike Tr

Turkey Tr

▶3.0

Bluff Road Tr

Start

Homestead Tr

Cutoff Tr

3.8▶

Ovenbird Tr

Middle Road Tr

Legend

- - main route
- - - other trail
— paved road
— dirt road
♨ waterfall
⊙ of interest

1500'
1300'
1100'

Lula Lake Falls

Lula Falls

Overlook

1 mi.   2 mi.   3 mi.   4 mi.

Glen Falls Trail

Hike Distance:	1.2 miles
Type of Hike:	Out & Back
Number of Falls:	3
Hiking Time:	1 hour
Dry Feet:	Yes
Start Elevation:	1,379 ft
Total Ascent:	300 ft
Land Manager:	NPS
Fee:	None

GLEN FALLS
Class: Sluice Height: 30 ft Rating: Good

Barely inside the Georgia line, on the flank of Lookout Mountain and within a stone's throw of Chattanooga, TN, this hike is like combining the popular tourist attractions of Ruby Falls and Rock City, albeit on a smaller scale. Like Ruby Falls, there is a waterfall (three, in fact), but not underground. And like Rock City, there is a place where the trail squeezes through a space in the rock.

Lookout Mountain is steeped in history—military history in particular. Considering the mountain's commanding view of the valley below, including the city of Chattanooga and the long sweep of the Tennessee River, this is not surprising. American Revolutionary War legend tells of a battle here between the forces of John Sevier and Chief Dragging Canoe of the Chickamaugas. However, the famed "Battle Above the Clouds," as the Battle of Lookout Mountain was known at the time, was a major turning point in the Civil War.

Over the course of a few days during September of 1863, the Confederate Army routed the Union troops at Chickamauga, GA, below

Lookout Mountain to the east. The Union, led by Major General William Rosecrans, retreated to Chattanooga, where they held the city. The Confederates, under the command of General Braxton Bragg, scaled Lookout Mountain, set up defenses, and began to besiege the city below. Rebel troops covered the very top of the mountain in addition to a relatively level area partway up, known as "the Bench." Above the Bench, cutting it off from the top, was an area of cliffs called the Palisades. On this hike you'll see that Glen Falls drops over the Palisades onto the Bench. The Bench proved to be the Confederates' downfall, because the topography was too steep for

the big guns. Artillery from above could not cover the area and left the Rebel soldiers unprotected. Using this advantage, the Union forces attacked under the cover of fog (thus the name "Battle Above the Clouds"), and the Rebels were handily defeated and forced to retreat into the foothills of north Georgia.

You know the rest of the story. Sherman and his Union troops swept down from the north and kept the Rebels on the run. Eventually he would burn Atlanta and then march to the sea, leaving scorched ground in his wake. Vital supply lines for the Confederates were cut and the weakened and demoralized South eventually surrendered.

Think about all this on your hike to the falls. What must it have been like for those men, hidden in the cloud of fog with bullets whizzing around them? Certainly the creek was a valuable source of much-needed water during the battle. Could the cliffs around the falls have made a great hideout, or was it in fact a death trap?

UPPER FALLS
Class: Tiered Height: 12 ft Rating: Fair

Glen Falls Trail (cont.)

Getting to the Trailhead

From Chattanooga, take Ochs Highway from St. Elmo up Lookout Mountain for 1.4 miles. Just beyond where Sanders Road enters from the right, park at the pulloff on the left. This is the trailhead.

From Lula Lake Land Trust, take Lula Lake Road north for 4.5 miles. Turn right on Red Ridinghood Lane at the 4-way stop. Continue down the mountain past Rock City as the road becomes Ochs Highway for 1.9 mile. Park at the pulloff on the right. A sign here says "Ruby Falls left 100 yd."

GPS Coordinates

N 34° 59.52' W 85° 20.45'

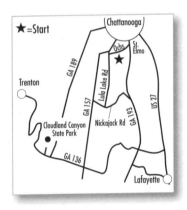

LOWER CASCADES (SECOND DROP)
Class: Tiered Height: 65 ft Rating: Good

and large rocks around the trail. The 30-foot Glen Falls drops into a pool just above a footbridge over the creek. Below it, the creek continues to drop in a series of 20- and 25-foot cascades. After viewing Glen Falls, continue across the bridge and turn hard to the right, up the stone steps and through "the squeeze," a natural hole through the rock cliff.

Mile 0.6 The trail continues alongside the stream above Glen Falls. Just before Ochs Highway is another very pretty 12-foot upper falls that ends in a staircase cascade leading down to Glen Falls. From here, return the way you came.

Mile 1.2 Finish.

Hiking Directions

Begin Walk down into the woods and onto Glen Falls Trail.

Mile 0.5 You are in a miniature Rock City here with high bluffs

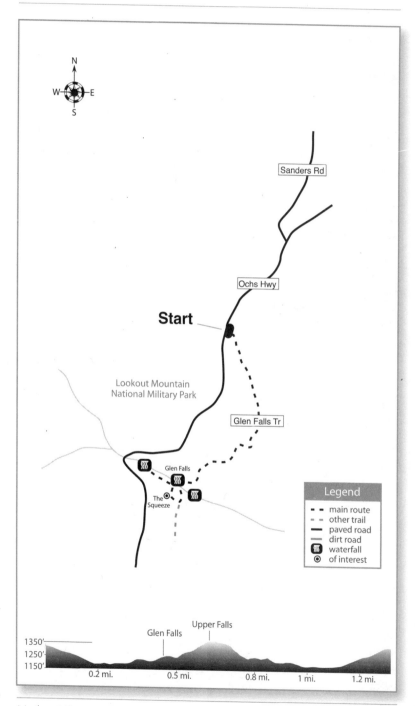

N
W · E
S

Sanders Rd

Ochs Hwy

Start

Lookout Mountain
National Military Park

Glen Falls Tr

Glen Falls

The
Squeeze

Legend
- – – main route
- – – other trail
- —— paved road
- —— dirt road
- ⌇ waterfall
- ⊙ of interest

Upper Falls

Glen Falls

1350'
1250'
1150'

0.2 mi.   0.5 mi.   0.8 mi.   1 mi.   1.2 mi.

Pocket Loop Trail

Hike Distance:	9.9 miles
Type of Hike:	Loop
Number of Falls:	1
Hiking Time:	Full day
Dry Feet:	Yes
Start Elevation:	909 ft
Total Ascent:	1,948 ft
Land Manager:	GA DNR
Fee:	None

POCKET BRANCH FALLS
Class: Horsetail Height: 50 ft Rating: Good

This is one of those hikes where, if you wanted to, you could just walk the short distance up to the falls, take a good look, turn around, head back to your car, and call it good. But remember, this is a hiking guide. Why turn back when such a good trail awaits?

Pigeon Mountain is one of Georgia's most interesting outdoor places. Lying like a thumb attached to the broad hand of Lookout Mountain, it shares the qualities of the larger plateau. Relatively flat on top and rimmed by limestone cliffs, it stands like a sentinel above the green valleys below. Outdoor enthusiasts of all stripes visit here. Hikers, mountain bikers, and equestrians share its trails most all the year round. Because it is a Georgia Department of Natural Resources Wildlife Management Area, hunters of deer, turkey, and small game attend special hunts here at various times during the game season.

High above the mountain, hang gliders soar from its high rocky outcrops while rock climbers try their skill on its many cliffs. Below ground, spelunkers continue to map out one of the East Coast's largest cave networks. On this hike you'll pass near the entrances to a couple of those caves. Given the geology of the mountain, chances are that much of the water that forms Pocket Branch itself, which bubbles up in a large spring just above the falls, flows through a cave long before reaching the surface.

Once you've passed Pocket Branch Falls, be prepared for a leg-burning climb. South Pocket Trail gradually works its way to the brow of Pigeon Mountain through an open hardwood forest. Along the way you'll pass numerous rock outcrops as the trail seeks a way to the top between high bluffs. It's almost a full three miles of climbing before you top out at the rim and join West Brow trail.

Once up on the brow, things ease up a bit as you skirt the clifftops on your way to what's called High Point, the highest spot on Pigeon Mountain. The clifftop views here are fabulous. Directly below you is the beautiful McLemore Cove, a place of green fields and old farmsteads. Across the cove you can see the rim of Lookout Mountain as it runs north towards Tennessee. It's a quiet spot where the only noise you'll hear is the wind in the trees,

maybe the whistle of a red-tailed hawk, or just your heart beating from the exertion of the climb.

Leaving High Point behind brings the welcome relief of walking downhill for a while, and then the variety of a few more ups and downs along the rim. As you approach the junction with Cane Trail, you'll be near the entrance to Ellison Cave. This is one of Pigeon Mountain's more notable caves, and you might even run into some spelunkers here.

Continuing onward on Pocket Loop Trail and with only one more rise to conquer, the main downhill portion of the trail soon begins. This is the section where you'll be glad you chose to wear your sturdiest hiking shoes. In places the trail is lovely and smooth, but in others you might wonder where all the water went, as it feels more like a streambed than a trail. Yes, this section of trail has an erosion problem—and, as with most downhills, it's over before you know it. You'll pass the falls a second time before returning to the trailhead.

Pocket Loop Trail (cont.)

Getting to the Trailhead

Take GA 193 west of LaFayette to Davis Crossroads and turn left onto Hogjowl Road. Go 2.7 miles and turn left onto Pocket Road. It's 1.3 more miles to the trailhead. **Caution:** Shallow stream ford on Pocket Road.

GPS Coordinates

N 34° 42.76' W 85° 22.80'

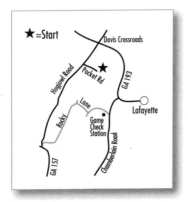

Hiking Directions

Begin From the trailhead parking area, go around the gate and follow the old roadbed up the hill.

Mile 0.4 Turn right off the old road toward the falls.

Mile 0.5 Waterfall. After viewing, turn back to old road and go right on up above the falls.

Mile 0.7 Just past the top of the falls, turn right on South Pocket Trail. You'll follow blue blazes up the mountain.

Mile 3.3 A sometimes rocky climb brings you to the top of the mountain. Turn left along the brow onto what is now Pocket Loop Trail. West Brow Trail has entered from the right and now follows the same path as Pocket Loop.

Mile 4.1 As you travel along the western brow of Pigeon Mountain you'll have amazing clifftop views of McLemore Cove below and Lookout Mountain ahead. Here you reach the high point of the hike—the spot called High Point.

Mile 5.2 Turn left on gravel roadbed as Atwood Trail enters from the right.

Mile 6.3 Bear left to continue on Pocket Loop Trail. West Brow and then Cane Trail exit to the right.

Mile 9.1 The trail down the mountain is rocky and rigorous. In places it shows heavy wear from horse users. You'll bottom out in a large meadow.

Mile 9.4 Look for a pond on the right and a large spring on the left. The water from this spring forms much of Pocket Branch Falls just below.

Mile 9.5 Close the loop. Continue on down the old roadbed, past the waterfall, and back to the trailhead.

Mile 9.9 Finish.

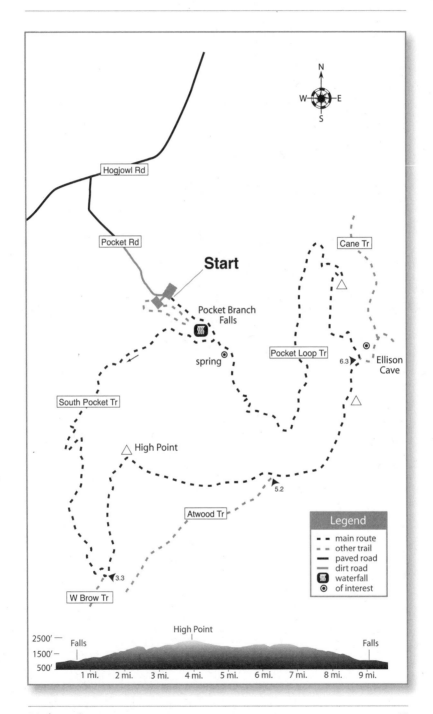

Hogjowl Rd

Pocket Rd

Start

Pocket Branch Falls

spring

South Pocket Tr

Cane Tr

Pocket Loop Tr

6.3

Ellison Cave

High Point

5.2

Atwood Tr

W Brow Tr

3.3

Legend

- - - main route
- - - other trail
—— paved road
—— dirt road
▨ waterfall
◉ of interest

2500' —
1500' —
500' —

Falls

High Point

Falls

1 mi. 2 mi. 3 mi. 4 mi. 5 mi. 6 mi. 7 mi. 8 mi. 9 mi.

Allen Creek Falls

Hike Distance:	6.4 miles
Type of Hike:	Loop
Number of Falls:	2
Hiking Time:	Half day
Dry Feet:	Maybe
Start Elevation:	1,906 ft
Total Ascent:	1,030 ft
Land Manager:	GA DNR
Fee:	None

ALLEN CREEK FALLS
Class: Tiered Height: 12 ft Rating: Fair

Just getting to the start of this hike is exciting. A very steep and twisty road leads you to Hood Overlook, high atop Pigeon Mountain's eastern brow. Be glad the road is paved—not so long ago it was dirt. Still, the tight turns and steep drop-offs can take your breath away. Once on top you'll find a spectacular view. Directly below is quiet and pastoral Shinbone Valley, where green fields are bordered by woods and interspersed with shimmering ponds. Far to the east, on a clear day, across the Great Valley you should be able to make out the faint outlines of Fort Mountain and the Cohuttas. Hang gliders frequently launch from here, and if you're lucky, you'll see them soaring on the updrafts created by the brow of the mountain you are standing on.

The trail that will take you to Allen Creek Falls is a meandering loop, all on top of the mountain. Several small streams cut into the otherwise flat-topped plateau; you must descend to cross each one and then climb up again. This makes for a hike that's hillier than you might guess.

Allen Creek Falls is a small but pretty waterfall at the head of what is called a gulf in these parts—a deep, wide chasm. The stream cuts a cleft in the mountain as it drops to the lower valley floor. In this case, vegetation on the steep slopes creates a hanging forest that fills in the cleft, but if you were a hawk flying high above, the outlines of the gulf would be easy to see.

The falls itself makes for a nice hiking destination and on this hike you'll get a double treat because a second, smaller falls on the Little East Fork of Allen Creek shares the same plunge pool. Don't expect to see many people here; this one is hardly what you'd call well known. If it's hot out, be sure to leave some time in your itinerary for a cooling dip; the pool is plenty deep enough. At both the top and the bottom of the falls you'll find large stone slabs, perfect for a lunch or snack break, or a sunny warm-up spot on a cool winter day.

The hike to and from the falls is a treat as well. The trails generally have a nice tread for easy walking, although some of the hilly sections tend to get washed out in places. You can expect to see huge boulders throughout the mixed hardwood forest—oak, hickory, maple, and sourwood.

Nearer the streams you'll find rhododendron, laurel, and azalea.

Toward the end of the hike you'll cross several large wildlife openings. Remember, this is first and foremost a wildlife management area. These fields are planted specifically with food for wildlife. If you approach these feeding areas quietly, the likelihood of spotting a deer or a flock of turkeys is greatly increased. Maybe you'll be lucky. Who knows what you'll see?

Little East Fork Falls
Class: Tiered Height: 10 ft Rating: Nice

Allen Creek Falls (cont.)

Getting to the Trailhead

From La Fayette, take GA 193 north 2.8 miles and turn left on Chamberlain Road. Go 3.5 miles and turn right on Rocky Lane. Continue past the check station up the mountain 3.6 miles and turn left on East Brow Road. Go 0.25 mile to the Hood Overlook trailhead. **Caution:** Rocky Lane is steep and roughly paved with several tight switchbacks.

GPS Coordinates

N 34° 39.13′ W 85° 22.38′

Hiking Directions

Begin From the trailhead follow the blue- and orange-blazed Hood/Atwood Trail out of the back of the parking area.

Mile 0.8 Turn left on blue-blazed Hood Trail. Orange-blazed Atwood continues to the right.

Mile 1.2 Two small streams come together here to form Allen Creek. Cross over to remain on

Hood Trail. A connector trail to Allen Creek Trail exits here to the left.

Mile 1.4 Gain the ridge here. A trail to a interesting rock formation area known as Rocktown exits right; stay left.

Mile 2.6 Turn left on Atwood Trail and cross Allen Creek. For a ways here, the trail and stream-bed share the same route.

Mile 2.8 Atwood Trail exits the old roadbed left here. Continue straight another 100 yards; Allen Creek Falls is down on the right, along with Little East Fork Falls. After viewing both of them, return the way you came in, turning right on Atwood Trail. In the next several miles you'll hike through open woods and several wildlife fields.

Mile 5.5 The connector trail you passed at mile 1.2 exits to the left here. Continue straight on Atwood Trail.

Mile 6.2 Go around gate and turn left on East Brow Road.

Mile 6.4 Finish.

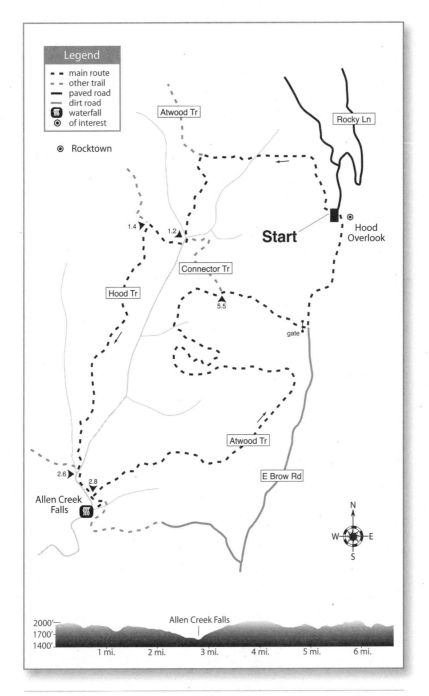

Legend
- main route
- other trail
- paved road
- dirt road
- waterfall
- of interest

⊙ Rocktown

Atwood Tr

Rocky Ln

Start

Hood Overlook

1.4

1.2

Connector Tr

5.5

Hood Tr

gate

Atwood Tr

E Brow Rd

2.6

2.8

Allen Creek Falls

N
W E
S

Allen Creek Falls

2000'
1700'
1400'

1 mi.   2 mi.   3 mi.   4 mi.   5 mi.   6 mi.

Keown Falls Trail

Hike Distance:	2/5 miles
Type of Hike:	Loop
Number of Falls:	2
Hiking Time:	Half day
Dry Feet:	Yes
Start Elevation:	1,013 ft
Total Ascent:	500/1,100 ft
Land Manager:	USFS
Fee:	None

KEOWN FALLS SOUTH
Class: Plunge Height: 25 ft Rating: Fair

Between Lookout Mountain to the west and the Cohuttas to the east is an area in northern Georgia known as the Great Valley. Rippling up on the western side of this valley are a series of high ridges with interesting names like Peavine Ridge, Taylors Ridge, Boynton Ridge, Horn Mountain, Rocky Face Mountain, Lavender Mountain, and Johns Mountain. In fact, geologists refer to this area as the Ridge and Valley region of the state. Here you'll find a small section of the Chattahoochee National Forest which protects the headwaters of Armuchee Creek, an area known as the Pocket, and Keown Falls Scenic Area.

The scenic area has two waterfalls, both identified on maps as Keown Falls. They are a short distance apart, on different branches of the stream before they merge, and fall over different sections of the same cliff. For the purposes of this hike let's call the first falls you'll come to Keown Falls North, and the second one Keown Falls South.

Please note that these small streams can all but dry up in the heat of summer. When you arrive at the trailhead, take a look at the stream just to the north of the parking area. If it is dry or has very little water, you can pretty much bet the falls will be dry, or just a drip at most. If water is flowing full and fast, the falls will be showing off their finest.

At Keown Falls Scenic Area you can choose from a couple of hikes—a short two-miler that takes in just the waterfalls, or a five-miler that includes the falls plus a loop around the top of Johns Mountain. The Johns Mountain section adds a bit more climbing, some spectacular views, and sections of trail that make it seem as if you're rockhopping on a dry stream bed.

Another nice thing about the five-miler is that you get to see Keown Falls North early in the hike and then again, along with Keown Falls South, later in the hike. If it's warm out, you'll have a chance to cool off before returning to your car. Both falls drop over the lip of a cliff, and the area behind them has been broken away by seasonal freezing and thawing. So what you get is a waterfall that acts like a shower—you can stand behind it and stay perfectly dry, or step out underneath it to get a refreshing bath.

Whichever you choose, be prepared for a climb to access each falls. Near Keown Falls North, the Forest Service has constructed a set of stone steps right up the side of the mountain. It's not far to the falls, but it's a steep climb. If you decide to do the two-mile hike, be sure to continue up the wooden steps just beyond Keown Falls North to the viewing platform just above it. It offers not only a great view of the Pocket, a high valley tucked between Johns Mountain and Horn Mountain, but also Horn Mountain itself to the east.

KEOWN FALLS NORTH
Class: Plunge Height: 35 ft Rating: Fair

Keown Falls Trail (cont.)

Getting to the Trailhead

From I-75 just north of Calhoun, take GA 136 to Villanow. Turn left on Pocket Road and drive 6.0 miles. Turn right on gravel FS 409 and continue 0.7 mile to Keown Falls Scenic Area picnic area and trailhead.

GPS Coordinates

N 34° 36.80' W 85° 05.30'

Hiking Directions

Begin From the trailhead, hike through the A-frame and onto the trail. You'll see both green (Keown Falls Trail) and white (Pinhoti Trail) blazes, as this section is shared by the two.

Mile 0.1 The trail splits here to begin the loop. Take the right fork, heading towards the overlook.

Mile 0.8 Just after a series of stone steps you'll reach Keown Falls North.

If you are doing the shorter, 2-mile hike: Continue by hiking directly behind the falls and along the base of the cliff another 0.2 mile to Keown Falls South, where you'll continue on down and back to the trailhead.

If you are doing the longer, 5-mile hike: Continue up the wooden steps to the viewing platform above Keown Falls North.

Mile 0.9 Turn right on Johns Mountain Trail.

Mile 1.7 Johns Mountain Overlook. There is a parking area here. Turn left to hike along the west brow of Johns Mountain.

Mile 3.9 Close the Johns Mountain Trail loop. Turn right down the steps to Keown Falls North. From here you'll follow the route of the 2-mile hike. Go behind the falls

JUST THE RIGHT FLOW FOR A SHOWER.

and along the base of the cliff.

Mile 4.2 Reach Keown Falls South. Continue past it and down the mountain.

Mile 4.9 Close the loop for the bottom loop trail. Turn right.

Mile 5.0 Finish.

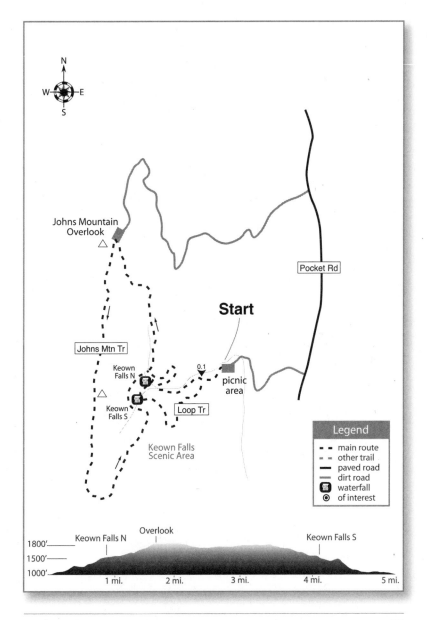

Cohutta Mountains

Upper Fifth Falls on Emery Creek

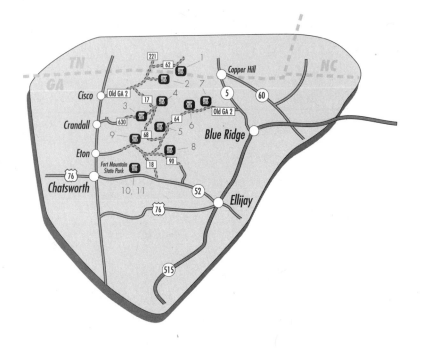

1. Beech Bottom Trail
2. Hickory Ridge–Rice Camp Loop
3. Mill Creek Falls
4. Panther Creek Falls
5. Conasauga–Chestnut Lead
6. Mountaintown Creek Trail
7. Shadow Falls
8. Pinhoti Trail
9. Emery Creek Trail
10. Gahutti–Cool Springs Loop
11. Gold Mine Creek Falls

What makes the Cohuttas stand apart from other mountains in Georgia? The key word here is remote. Stepping onto most any of the trails in this section means you're stepping into wilderness. Four of these hikes lie within the Cohutta Wilderness Area itself. In the woods around Mountaintown or Emery Creek, you'll feel so far from civilization, you might as well be in a designated wilderness.

The Cohutta Wilderness Area was one of the first to be established in the entire eastern United States. Sixteen wilderness areas were created when Congress passed the Wilderness Act in 1975. At the time, the Cohutta was the largest of them all, at over 34,000 acres.

The act states, "Wilderness is an area where the earth and its community of life are untrammeled by man, where man himself is a visitor who does not remain." In a designated wilderness, trails typically go unblazed and unmarked. Motorized equipment of any sort is banned. This means downed trees can't be removed with a chainsaw, and any trail repair must be done with hand tools—no backhoes allowed.

Here you'll find black bear, wild boar, and over 40 species of rare plants. You'll also find two major mountain rivers and quite a few waterfalls, several in the spectacular category.

Surrounding and protecting the wilderness area is a huge buffer zone of near-wilderness enclosed by the Chattahoochee National Forest. This tract, crisscrossed by a network of dirt forest roads and foot trails, includes mountains that rise to over 3,500 feet. If you're looking for a place to camp before an early morning hike, you'll also find some pretty little Forest Service campgrounds, several free of charge.

Anchoring the southwest corner of the Cohuttas is Fort Mountain, topped by Fort Mountain State Park. Compared to the National Forest and the Wilderness Area, you'll find the state park to be rather plush—with cabins, a developed campground, and a network of groomed, well-maintained trails. Of course there are waterfalls here, too.

One important rule for hiking in the Cohuttas: Allow plenty of time to get to the trailhead. Except for Fort Mountain State Park, every hike requires a long drive on hilly, curvy, sometimes rugged gravel mountain roads.

FIRST FALLS ON BIRCH CREEK

Beech Bottom Trail

Hike Distance:	8.9 miles
Type of Hike:	Lollipop
Number of Falls:	2
Hiking Time:	3/4 day
Dry Feet:	No
Start Elevation:	1,564 ft
Total Ascent:	1,069 ft
Land Manager:	USFS
Fee:	None

LOWER JACKS RIVER FALLS
Class: Cataract Height: 80 ft Rating: Spectacular

Jacks River Falls is probably the most popular destination in the Cohutta Wilderness, and of the several ways to get there, this is the easiest one. That doesn't mean this hike is easy, just that it's easier than other routes. Jacks River Falls itself is huge, gorgeous, and remote—no wonder it's popular. Its thundering noise alone commands attention. Start this hike on a quiet, windless day and you'll be able to hear the falls soon after leaving your car. The sound begins almost as a whisper, so soft you're not sure if it's the falls you're hearing or something else. As you get closer, it becomes a little more definite. The sound gets louder, and you begin to pick out a constant and distinctive low drone. When you drop behind a ridge you lose it, but as you get a little closer, the drone becomes a soft roar. All this when you're still miles away. Once you're in the area just below the falls, the roar is so loud you have to shout to be heard.

Walking to Jacks River Falls on the Beech Bottom Trail is not all about sounds. The trail itself follows the route of an old roadbed dating back to when people actually lived on small farms down in the "bottoms." Its fairly gentle grade makes for good walking. Along the way you'll pass the occasional monster hemlock, oak, or hickory, with an understory of mountain laurel, flame azalea, and rhododendron.

Once you've made it down to Beech Bottom and the Jacks River, the walking gets a little rougher, but just a bit. This is due mostly to any scrambling around on the rocks you do to get down to the falls. If it's warm, this is definitely a place to take a swim or cool your feet. The extra-large pool at the bottom of the second falls makes a great swimming hole. Don't be surprised if you run into other folks here; it is a popular area. Still, to get here and back is a nine-mile hike, which tends to weed out most of the casual walker crowd. Should you decide to make this into an overnight excursion (plenty of folks do), be aware that camping is not allowed at Beech Bottom or anywhere close to the falls. Signs should be posted at the trailhead denoting the exact camping boundaries.

Even though Jacks River Falls is most definitely in Georgia, you'll start and end this hike in Tennessee. And although this is the easiest *hike* to the falls, it's still a challenge to drive to. You'll travel for close to 13 miles on winding, dusty dirt and gravel Forest Service–maintained roads to get to the trailhead, so be sure to factor in a little extra travel time on either end of your hike, and make sure your tank is full of gas.

Bonus Falls

STAIRSTEP FALLS
Class: Tiered Height: 30 ft
Rating: Good

You'll pass Stairstep Falls 0.7 mile north of Jacks River Bridge on FS 221 en route to the trailhead. This pretty low-flow stream falls is on a small tributary of Sheeds Creek. You'll see it just off the east side of the road, where there is a convenient pulloff for viewing.

Beech Bottom Trail (cont.)

Getting to the Trailhead

From Cisco on US 411, take Old GA 2 to the Jacks River Bridge, 8.7 miles. Bear right onto FS 221, go 1.2 miles and turn right on FS 62. Continue another 5.7 miles, and the Beech Bottom trailhead will be on the left.

GPS Coordinates

N 34° 59.43' W 84° 35.30'

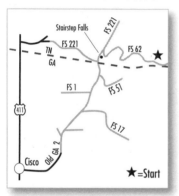

Hiking Directions

Begin From the trailhead parking lot, cross the road to the sign-board and continue past it and onto the trail.

Mile 3.4 Bottom out at Beech Bottom. It's a little confusing here because the creek has washed out the trail. You'll need to ford the creek and continue on the trail on the other side, going away from the creek.

Mile 4.0 After going up and over a small hill you'll come to the Jacks River. Turn right on Jacks River Trail and walk downstream.

Mile 4.5 Ford Beech Creek again onto the bare rock on the other side. You should hear the roar of the falls just below. Continue down the righthand side of the river.

Mile 4.6 Reach upper Jacks River Falls. You can scramble down the rocks to the pool just below the upper falls. A giant stone slab beside the water makes a nice spot to take a break, eat a snack, or eat lunch. To get to the bottom of lower Jacks River Falls, go back up to the trail and follow it along the right side as it goes high above the falls. Once past the drop you can scramble down to the water via one of the several goatpaths visitors have created over the years. When you're ready for the return hike, work your way back to mile 4.5. Cross Beech Creek and turn left, then follow the creek back to mile

UPPER JACKS RIVER FALLS
Class: Tiered Height: 12 ft Rating: Good

3.4, fording the stream in several places. This is different from the way you came in alongside Jacks River. When you arrive back at Beech Bottom, turn left on Beech Bottom Trail and return the way you came.

Mile 8.9 Finish.

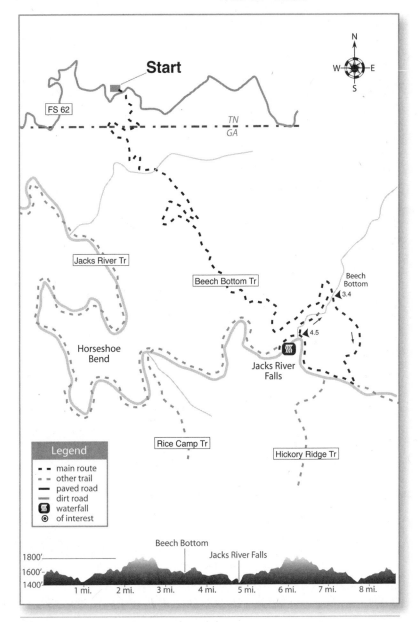

Hickory Ridge-Rice Camp Loop

Hike Distance:	11.6 miles
Type of Hike:	Loop
Number of Falls:	3+
Hiking Time:	Full day
Dry Feet:	No
Start Elevation:	1,777 ft
Total Ascent:	2,826 ft
Land Manager:	USFS
Fee:	None

LOWER JACKS RIVER FALLS
Class: Cataract Height: 80 ft Rating: Spectacular

No bones about it, this is a long and difficult day hike. You'll travel deep into the heart of the Cohutta Wilderness and see some of Georgia's most remote territory. It's every bit worth the effort. Once back in your car and heading home, you'll forget that first three-mile climb that seemed to go on forever. You'll forget how many times you crossed a stream (no fewer than 20). You'll forget that slopping-along feeling of hiking in wet footwear and that wide, slippery river crossing. You'll forget that steep downhill where your knees screamed and you were looking for a tree to grab should gravity take over entirely. Well, you may not forget it if gravity won out and you missed the tree. Nevertheless, the difficult elements of this hike will become faint memories soon enough.

What will you likely remember? That awesome feeling when you reached the top of Hickory Ridge and traversed its knife-like spine. The first time you knew for sure you were hearing Jacks River Falls roaring somewhere off in the distance. Those views of endless ridges with not a sign of humankind. The thundering power of a wilderness river as it crashes first over one falls and then another before pounding down a gorge over numerous smaller falls, each of which alone would be a single destination but are dwarfed by big brother just upstream. Who could forget the large plunge pool that seems ready-made for swimming and lolling about in the warm sunshine, or the perfect lunch spot on big slabs of rock between the two falls?

Yes, this is a great hike, but there are some things you'll need to be aware of before heading out. The first is the lengthy drive to the trailhead. From Cisco, you'll drive 10 long miles on roads that become progressively curvy and bumpy. Toward the end you'll have to make two stream fords in your vehicle. These can be a foot or more deep, so make sure beforehand that your car will clear them. Also, if these streams are running deep and fast from heavy rains, consider going another day. The condition of this stream is a good indicator of what the crossings on Jacks River may be like later on during your hike, and you certainly don't want to risk crossing the Jacks in flood. Better to turn back while still in your car. You'd still have time to hike down to the falls via Beech Bottom Trail (p. 58).

There's plenty of history on this hike. Starting out you'll follow what the topo maps say is the old roadbed of the original Georgia Highway 2. As rugged and steep as it is, it's hard to believe travelers made very good time on it. In the Jacks River Gorge, you'll follow the remains of an abandoned logging railroad. You can still see where the mountainside was dynamited to make a level railbed.

RICE CAMP CREEK FALLS
Class: Tiered   Height: 8 ft   Rating: Nice

Hickory Ridge-Rice Camp Loop (cont.)

Getting to the Trail

From Cisco on US 411, take Old GA 2 eight miles to Cottonwood Patch Campground. Turn right here on FS 51 and drive another 4.8 miles to the end of the road and trailhead. **Caution**: Two big stream fords on FS 51.

GPS Coordinates

N 34° 57.02' W 84° 36.31'

★ =Start

Hiking Directions

Begin From the trailhead, head uphill on East Cowpen Trail. The trail forks almost immediately. Continue on left fork.

Mile 2.7 After a long and some-times steep climb, you'll finally gain the top of the ridge. Turn left onto Hickory Ridge Trail.

Mile 5.9 A steep downhill brings you to Jacks River. Cross to the other side (this can be a deep ford; scouting up or downstream may provide better options), and turn left on Jacks River Trail.

Mile 6.2 Ford Beech Creek; Jacks River Falls is just below. You can view the upper falls by scrambling down to the rock slabs beside the plunge pool. To reach the plunge pool of the lower (and much taller) falls, follow the trail as it skirts the right side high above the falls. Access the bottom pool by any of several user-created goatpaths. The route continues down the right side of the river.

Mile 7.5 Ford Jacks River (use

Bonus Falls

JIGGER CREEK FALLS
Class: Tiered Height: 30 ft
Rating: Good

You'll pass Jigger Creek Falls en route to the trailhead. Start looking for it off the right side of the road 1.7 miles after you've turned onto FS 51 after leaving Cottonwood Patch Campground. If you get to the stream ford and have not spotted it, you've gone 0.3 mile too far. There is a small pulloff just above the falls.

caution; this one is really slippery), and bear right where you'll cross a small stream. Continue downstream another 100 yards, and turn left on Rice Camp Trail.

Mile 10.5 Many stream cross-ings later and just off the trail to the right is the small Rice Camp Creek Falls. It sits just above a rocky bluff.

Mile 11.6 Finish.

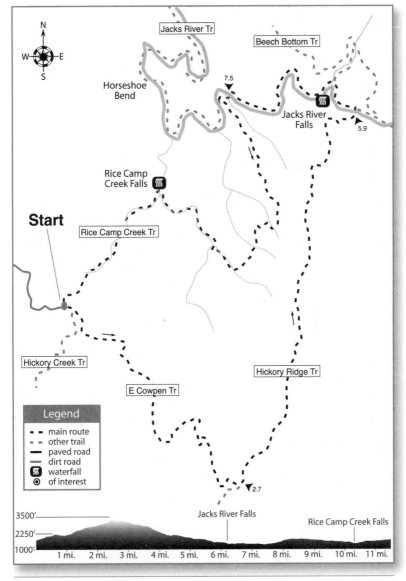

Mill Creek Falls

Hike Distance:	1.2 miles
Type of Hike:	Out & Back
Number of Falls:	4+
Hiking Time:	1 hour +
Dry Feet:	Yes
Start Elevation:	1,807 ft
Total Ascent:	266 ft
Land Manager:	USFS
Fee:	None

THIRD FALLS ON MILL CREEK
Class: Slide/Tiered Height: 80 ft Rating: Excellent

This is a short hike with a big payoff. In just over a mile's walk, you'll view four beautiful waterfalls. The largest of the bunch nears 80 feet in height while the rest are 10, 20, and 75 feet. Who would guess when driving on flat, boring US 411 between Chatsworth and Crandall that such scenery is so close at hand?

Scenic Mill Creek flows from the edge the Cohutta Wilderness Area, beginning at Lake Conasauga, high up in the hills. It's popular as a wild trout fishing destination, so don't be surprised to run into an angler or two on your hike. Many of the people who come to camp at Hickey Gap are here to fish. Another activity you might be surprised to see, here of all places, is whitewater kayaking. "Surely you jest," you say. "There's an 80-foot waterfall!" But paddling Mill Creek falls into the category of—to use boating lingo—"steep creekin'." Creek boaters, as they are known, look for small streams with lots of gradient which, after heavy rains, have enough water to float their short six- to nine-foot boats. Waterfalls such as these, with deep pools at the bottom, are considered "runable," and Mill Creek is quite the challenge. So, heads up for anything in the bright-colored plastic category that may come screaming over the lip while you're setting up for the perfect photo. It's rare, but it happens.

Another nice feature of Mill Creek is the six-site Hickey Gap USFS Campground where you start and end your hike. It's small, quiet, clean, and currently fee-free for camping. You can expect picnic tables, pit toilets, and level tent sites. Should you be planning a hike to Panther Creek Falls in the Cohutta Wilderness Area (p. 70) and want to get an early start, this campground makes a good place to spend the night,

SECOND FALLS ON MILL CREEK
Class: Block Height: 10 ft Rating: Fair

reducing the amount of time it takes to drive up to the Wilderness boundary. The option of a short hike down to view the falls on Mill Creek the night before is an added bonus.

FIRST FALLS ON MILL CREEK Class: Tiered
Height: 75 ft over 50 yd Rating: Good

Mill Creek Falls (cont.)

Getting to the Trailhead

From Crandall on US 411, go east on Grassy Street. Cross the railroad tracks and turn right on Crandall Ellijay Road and immediately left onto Mill Creek Road. This road becomes FS 630 when you enter the national forest. Continue another 4.0 miles to Hickey Gap Campground. The trail begins at the lower right end of the campground.

GPS Coordinates

N 34° 53.63' W 84° 40.26'

FOURTH FALLS ON MILL CREEK
Class: Tiered Slide Height: 20 ft Rating: Fair

following is the third falls. It is very high, starting with a 30-foot slide and then cascading another 50 feet into a deep plunge pool.

Mile 0.6 You'll have to scramble down a steep slope where roots and sketchy ropes give you handholds to the plunge pool for the third falls. It's a great swimming hole and hangout spot.

Mile 0.6+ Less than 0.1 mile downstream is the fourth and final falls of this short tour—a 20-foot steep slide ending in a near-vertical drop. Return the way you came, taking care on the climb up past the third falls.

Mile 1.2 Finish.

Hiking Directions

Begin You'll see the creek on the far side of the campground. Walk toward it and then down the right shore. The trail is not marked, but it is well defined.

Mile 0.1 Here is the first falls, long and tiered, stretching for 50 yards and dropping 75 feet.

Mile 0.5 Second falls. Easily recognizable as a block-type dropping 10 feet. Immediately

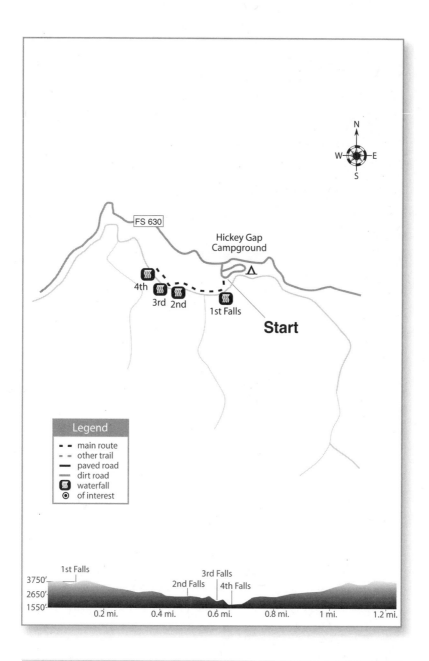

FS 630

Hickey Gap
Campground

4th

3rd 2nd

1st Falls

Start

Legend
- - main route
- - other trail
— paved road
— dirt road
🌊 waterfall
⊙ of interest

3750'
2650'
1550'

1st Falls

2nd Falls

3rd Falls

4th Falls

0.2 mi.   0.4 mi.   0.6 mi.   0.8 mi.   1 mi.   1.2 mi.

Panther Creek Falls

Hike Distance:	10.6 miles
Type of Hike:	Out & Back
Number of Falls:	1
Hiking Time:	Full day
Dry Feet:	No
Start Elevation:	2,376 ft
Total Ascent:	2,254 ft
Land Manager:	USFS
Fee:	None

PANTHER CREEK FALLS
Class: Tiered Height: 450 ft Rating: Spectacular

There are at least two Panther Creek Falls in Georgia. This hike takes you to the one farthest to the west. You'll find it smack in the middle of the southern portion of the Cohutta Wilderness, and getting to it from any direction is a job. Although this may not be the absolute shortest route, it's probably the least difficult. It's also a very scenic and fun hike.

Starting high on the western slope of the wilderness area, you'll begin by hiking down an old roadbed that is the southern end of the Hickory Creek Trail. Although it's pretty dry up on the ridge, soon you'll begin to hear the sound of crashing water from somewhere down in the rhododendron bushes. For a waterfall hike, this is always a good sound. Many footsteps later you begin to get glimpses of the white blur that is the creek far below. Certainly there are waterfalls down there, but you'd need a rope to see for yourself. In this case, just hearing and imagining them is good.

Eventually you'll bottom out and begin a very pleasant walk alongside the upper Conasauga River. This is a trout fisherman's paradise. There are miles of unspoiled waters full of fish, and for the hiker it's a real treat, too.

Sandy river beaches beside idyllic green pools invite you to pull off your shoes and stay a while. You've got a ways to go, though, so don't tarry too long.

One interesting thing you'll see along the way is the remains of an old beaver pond. There is no pond there now, but you should recognize it when you pass the flat, open, marshy place where the trail ventures away from the river.

Beyond the old beaver pond marsh you'll return to the river and come to what appears to be a very large campsite. It is—but it's also the site of an old homestead. Imagine living here year round. What a spot—so quiet, and a long way from anywhere.

Once on the Panther Creek trail, things get really interesting. For one, you begin to climb, steadily at first, then more steeply. Before long the trail barely clings to the hillside, and still you climb. One last creek crossing and the trail disappears into a near-vertical boulder garden. Don't be dismayed, it's really not a difficult climb. The scattered boulders act like steps. Just off to your right is the lower portion of Panther Creek Falls, much of it hidden in the rhodo, but the energy and the crashing sound is there to urge you upward. As you climb higher still, the waterfall reveals itself. The falls' top portion drops straight over a high cliff. Stay on the trail and you'll soon find yourself up at the very lip of the falls for a top-of-Georgia view.

SHOALS AND GREEN POOL ON UPPER CONASAUGA RIVER

Panther Creek Falls (cont.)

Getting to the Trailhead

From Crandall on US 411, go east on Grassy Street. Cross the railroad tracks and turn right on Crandall Ellijay Road, then immediately left onto Mill Creek Road. This road becomes FS 630 when you enter the national forest. Continue another 6.2 miles past Hickey Gap Campground at the junction of FS 17. Stay on FS 630 another 0.3 mile to the trailhead.

GPS Coordinates

N 34° 54.11' W 84° 38.60'

Hiking Directions

Begin From the trailhead, hike downhill on Hickory Creek Trail.

Mile 1.7 Junction of Conasauga River and Conasauga River Trail. Bear right along the river on Hickory Creek Trail/Conasauga River Trail.

Mile 2.5 Pass remains of old beaver pond.

Mile 3.0 Enter large open area. Hickory Creek Trail fords the river here. Don't cross, but turn right and in a short distance Tearbritches Trail will exit uphill to the right. Don't take it either. Continue across a small stream, follow the trail up a short hill, and then return to the river.

Mile 3.9 Turn left and ford the river onto Panther Creek Trail. You will now begin to ascend alongside Panther Creek. It gets quite exciting the farther up you go.

Mile 5.0 Cross Panther Creek below a cascade. This is the absolute bottom of Panther Creek Falls. From here to the top of the falls, the trail climbs steeply through a boulder garden. Keep your eye peeled for trail blazes and remember—as long as the creek is to your right and you are climbing, that's good. Near the top, you'll see that the trail climbs

VIEW FROM PANTHER CREEK FALLS

through a cleft in the cliff that forms the falls. Blazes guide the way, but if you miss them, look for a break in the cliff a few hundred feet to the left of the falls.

Mile 5.3 Finally—the top! Expect

a great view here and a nice place for a break right at the lip of the falls. Return the way you came, taking care going down through the boulder field.

Mile 10.6 Finish.

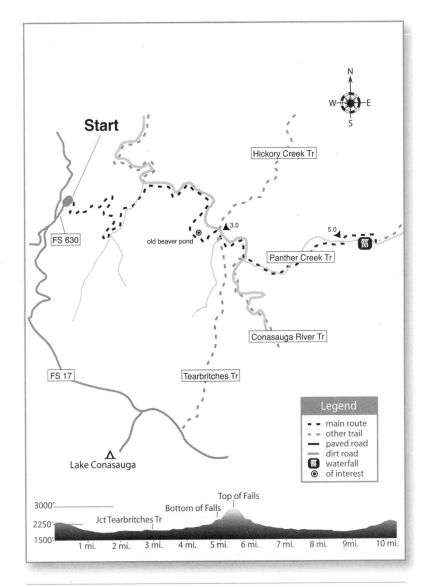

Conasauga-Chestnut Lead

Hike Distance:	5.4 miles
Type of Hike:	Out & Back
Number of Falls:	7
Hiking Time:	Half day
Dry Feet:	No
Start Elevation:	3,149 ft
Total Ascent:	1,358 ft
Land Manager:	USFS
Fee:	None

FIRST FALLS ON BIRCH CREEK
Class: Sluice Height: 10 ft Rating: Fair

Plan to do this hike in early spring, sometime around mid-April. You'll be glad you did. Aside from the seven small waterfalls, the wildflowers that bloom along the entire stretch at this season are amazing. Every turn of the trail brings a different assortment of colors. In places, the entire forest floor is carpeted with many varieties of flowers. In greatest abundance are trillium and trout lilies. Interspersed among these are violets of all kinds and colors. You might see young ramps and the occasional showy orchis. Later in the spring look for azalea, rhododendron, and mountain laurel. Just call this a waterfall and wildflower hike.

Waterfalls are here aplenty. None are what you'd call overly large, but they are good examples of what you're likely to find on many high elevation streams. The first three are on Birch Creek, a headwater stream for the Conasauga River. All are off the trail and hidden in the bushes, but if you're persistent, you'll find them. If you're one who likes sticking to the trail, you can enjoy hearing them crashing along. There are three more small falls on Chestnut Lead, right beside the trail. Finally, you'll see the uppermost falls on the Conasauga River just below where Chestnut Lead enters the stream and the Conasauga begins.

If you look up and away from the creeks for a moment, you'll also notice, especially on Chestnut Lead, some absolutely huge hemlocks. These monsters tower so high you have to crane your neck to see their tops. To reach all the way around one, you'll need at least one other person. Unfortunately, you may not have long to enjoy them. Unless conditions change drastically, they are doomed. A terminal infestation has been killing off our hemlocks from north to south at an alarming rate (for details, see p. 245). The ones here in Georgia wait silently while their kin as close as North Carolina

SECOND FALLS ON CHESTNUT LEAD
Class: Sluice Height: 10 ft Rating: Fair

are dying off. Researchers are trying desperately to save what they can, using everything from insecticides to predatory beetles. But the number of trees makes the job overwhelming. Mostly they're just attempting to buy time, hoping some hemlocks will develop a natural defense. Let's hope something works.

FIRST FALLS ON CONASAUGA RIVER
Class: Tiered Height: 20 ft Rating: Good

Conasauga-Chestnut Lead (cont.)

Getting to the Trailhead

From Milepost 8 on GA 52 west of Ellijay, take Gates Chapel Road 5.4 miles. Continue onto FS 90 for another 1.7 miles and turn right on FS 68. Drive 3.3 miles and turn right on FS 64, then go 1.4 miles the Conasauga River trailhead.

GPS Coordinates
N 34° 51.28' W 84° 34.87'

Hiking Directions

Begin Walk down Conasauga River Trail into the wilderness area.

Mile 1.2 The small but pretty first and second falls on Birch Creek are down off the trail to your right. Begin listening for them once you start down a fairly steep stretch of trail. You'll have to bushwhack through the rhodo to see them; listen for the loudest crashing water and follow the sound.

Mile 1.3 The third falls on Birch Creek is below the trail to your right. This one is more difficult to get to than the first and second. Start listening for it when you're about halfway down the steep section.

Mile 1.9 Junction of Conasauga Trail and Chestnut Lead Trail. The first falls on the Conasauga River is just beyond here on the other side of the campsite and right off the trail. To continue, ford the river onto Chestnut Lead Trail.

Mile 2.0 Pass third falls on Chestnut Lead.

Mile 2.6 Pass second falls on Chestnut Lead.

Bonus Falls

BARNES CREEK FALLS
Class: Segmented Height: 25 ft
Rating: Good

As you drive to the trailhead, look for this pretty waterfall 1.0 mile up FS 68 on the right side of the road. There's a picnic table and viewing platform here as well.

Mile 2.7 First falls on Chestnut Lead. The trail gets noticeably steeper here and it's a good place to turn around. Retrace your steps to the start.

Mile 5.4 Finish.

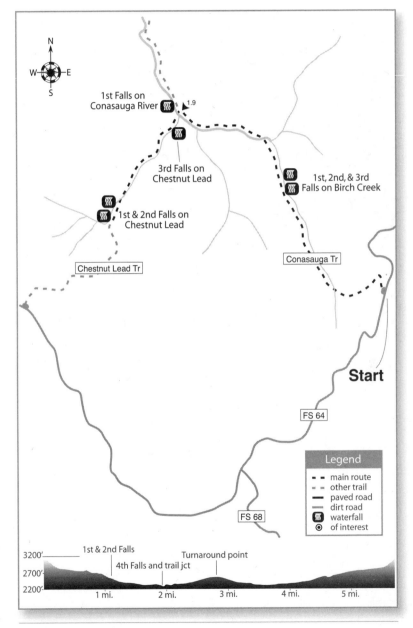

1st Falls on Conasauga River 1.9

3rd Falls on Chestnut Lead

1st, 2nd, & 3rd Falls on Birch Creek

1st & 2nd Falls on Chestnut Lead

Chestnut Lead Tr

Conasauga Tr

Start

FS 64

Legend
- - main route
- - other trail
— paved road
— dirt road
🌊 waterfall
◉ of interest

FS 68

3200'
2700'
2200'

1st & 2nd Falls

4th Falls and trail jct

Turnaround point

1 mi. 2 mi. 3 mi. 4 mi. 5 mi.

Mountaintown Creek Trail

Hike Distance:	8 miles
Type of Hike:	Out & Back
Number of Falls:	4+
Hiking Time:	Half day
Dry Feet:	No
Start Elevation:	3,165 ft
Total Ascent:	1,700 ft
Land Manager:	USFS
Fee:	None

FIRST FALLS ON CRENSHAW CREEK
Class: Tiered Height: 10 ft Rating: Fair

It's possible to get to this impressive series of waterfalls from a couple of different directions. This particular route brings you in from the top, where you'll walk along the stream as it builds from a small branch to a raging torrent. If you're already up on FS 64, and maybe you've just done the short hike to Shadow Falls (p. 82), this is a good option. If you enjoy long drives on remote forest roads with outstanding views, again, it's a good option. On the other hand, if you want to shorten your driving time, try hiking in from the bottom (see Pinhoti Trail hike, p. 84). Be aware that the road to this trailhead is closed in January and February.

This hike begins high on FS 64, a gravel road that traverses the ridges bordering the Cohutta Wilderness Area, following the route of Old Georgia Highway 2. Once off the road and on the trail, you'll quickly leave the ridgetops as you descend into the Mountaintown Creek watershed, where you'll begin rockhopping and wading Crenshaw Creek. A little over a mile and a half into the hike, the waterfalls begin. The first two are easily seen from the trail, one right after the other. What follows is unique to hiking trails in north Georgia. For close to half a mile, the stream crashes, boils, sluices, and slides in one continuous cascade. For all but the most ambitious waterfall buffs, the experience is more auditory than visual. The water runs through a tight, rhododendron-filled, precipitous chasm, the foot trail passing high above it. Unless you make some daring, tree-grabbing descents, you'll see only splashes of a whitewater ribbon through the forest. Still, the reverberating sounds of crashing water are dramatic and exciting.

SECOND FALLS ON CRENSHAW CREEK
Class: Tiered Height: 30 ft Rating: Good

Things quiet down a bit until you near the turnaround point and the lowest waterfall—a pretty one in the fair category.

A small, well-used campsite marks the spot for turning back. Here Heddy Branch joins Crenshaw to form Mountaintown Creek. If you've brought a lunch or snack, this is a good place to refuel for the climb out. Or maybe you found some kind soul willing to drop you off at the top of the hike and pick you up at the bottom. In that case, just pick up the directions from Pinhoti Trail hike mile 3.5 (p. 86) , and you'll be on your merry way.

START OF HIGH CASCADES
Class: Sluice Height: 100+ ft Rating: Excellent

Mountaintown Creek Trail (cont.)

Getting to the Trailhead

From Milepost 8 on GA 52 west of Ellijay, take Gates Chapel Road 5.4 miles. Continue onto FS 90 for another 1.7 miles and turn right on FS 68. Drive 3.3 miles and turn right on FS 64, then go 6.9 miles to the Mountaintown Creek trailhead parking lot. Or follow directions to Shadow Falls on p. 82 and continue another 2.0 miles on FS 64 to the trailhead.

GPS Coordinates

N 34° 52.30' W 84° 32.42'

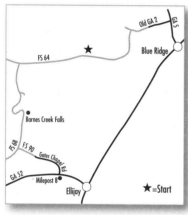

MIDDLE OF HIGH CASCADES   Class: Sluice
Height: 100+ ft Rating: Excellent

the next half-mile. The trail itself stays high to the right side as the cascades crash down through the rhodo far below. From the trail you should catch glimpses of frothing whitewater.

Mile 3.7 Off to the left of the trail is the lower falls on Crenshaw, a 10-foot tiered drop.

Mile 4.0 You'll find an established campsite here as Heddy Branch enters from the right. This is a good place to turn around.

Mile 8.0 Finish.

Hiking Directions

Begin Walk down and across FS 64 onto Mountaintown Creek Trail.

Mile 1.8 The first and second falls on Crenshaw Creek are down off the trail to your right.

Mile 2.2 The High Cascades begin here and continue for

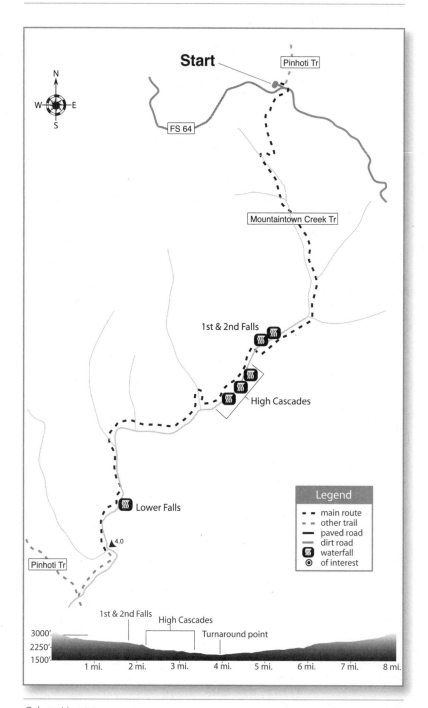

Start

Pinhoti Tr

FS 64

Mountaintown Creek Tr

1st & 2nd Falls

High Cascades

Lower Falls

▲4.0

Pinhoti Tr

Legend
- - - main route
- - - other trail
—— paved road
—— dirt road
🌊 waterfall
⊙ of interest

1st & 2nd Falls

High Cascades

Turnaround point

3000'
2250'
1500'

1 mi. 2 mi. 3 mi. 4 mi. 5 mi. 6 mi. 7 mi. 8 mi.

Shadow Falls

Hike Distance:	1 mile
Type of Hike:	Out & Back
Number of Falls:	1
Hiking Time:	1 hour
Dry Feet:	Yes
Start Elevation:	2,686 ft
Total Ascent:	150 ft
Land Manager:	USFS
Fee:	None

SHADOW FALLS
Class: Tiered Height: 25 ft Rating: Good

This is a short hike to a good waterfall, and much more level than the elevation profile makes it appear. The trail is an old roadbed shared with horses and bikes. At the falls, a steep goatpath takes you down to a shady plunge pool, plenty deep enough for a swim. Take care on the climb down; it can be slippery and you might end up swimming whether you want to or not.

Consider staying at the quaint Jacks River Fields campground ($5 fee) and checking out this falls early before heading up to Mountaintown Creek Trail and its High Cascades (p. 78), or saving it until the end of the day. It's a long drive here for just this one waterfall, so combining it with another hike is a good idea.

Getting to the Trailhead

From Blue Ridge, take GA 5 north for 3.7 miles, turn left on Old GA 2, and continue another 10.5 miles to Watson Gap. Turn left on FS 64 for 4.0 miles to Jacks River Fields Campground. The trail begins on the right, just before the campground entrance. Or follow directions to Mountaintown Creek on p. 80 and continue another 2.0 miles on FS 64.

GPS Coordinates
N 34° 51.85' W 84° 31.19'

Hiking Directions

Begin Walk out of the campground, down the road, cross the river, and turn left on South Fork Trail.

Mile 0.5 You should hear and see the falls. A small goatpath leads down to the plunge pool. Return the way you came. If you want to continue down the trail, in another 0.2 mile you'll reach the northern terminus of the long-distance Pinhoti Trail, which begins in Alabama and connects here to the Benton MacKaye Trail.

Mile 1.0 Finish.

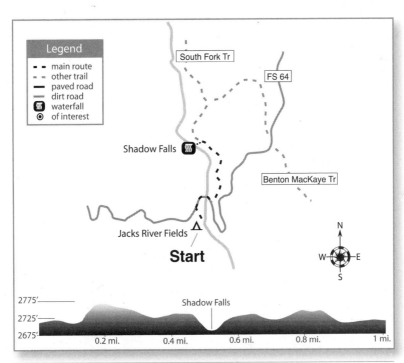

Pinhoti Trail

Hike Distance:	11.4 miles
Type of Hike:	Out & Back
Number of Falls:	4+
Hiking Time:	Full day
Dry Feet:	No
Start Elevation:	1,794 ft
Total Ascent:	1,800 ft
Land Manager:	USFS
Fee:	None

HIGH CASCADES ON CRENSHAW CREEK
Class: Sluice Height: 100+ ft Rating: Excellent

This is the lower, longer, somewhat more difficult hike to the High Cascades on Crenshaw Creek (see Mountaintown Creek Trail, p. 78), but it offers an easier drive into the trailhead. On this route you'll encounter more diversity in terrain on a number of different trails, and there are interesting things to see along the way.

All but half a mile of the hike follows the course of Pinhoti Trail. This long-distance, multi-use trail begins in Alabama and continues for 240 miles, ending not too many more miles beyond the turnaround point of this hike. The Pinhoti is a relatively new trail, the purpose of which is to link the southernmost Appalachian Mountains in Alabama with the Appalachian National Scenic Trail (AT). It accomplishes.this by connecting to the Benton MacKaye Trail, which then leads to the AT. Most of the route is on footpaths, but there are some sections that follow roads. The Keown Falls Trail hike (p. 50) also follows a section of the Pinhoti.

A short distance into this hike you'll pass the Gennett Poplar, Georgia's largest tulip poplar tree. Standing well over 100 feet high and with a circumference that takes numerous pairs of arms to reach around, this is one big tree.

Just beyond the big tree, you'll begin the first of several huffer-puffer climbs, working your way by trails and old roadbeds up and over the ridge separating Bear Creek from Mountaintown Creek. Notice the changes in trees and other vegetation as you leave the wet areas, climb to the dry ridges, and return to the streams again.

Heading upstream alongside Mountaintown Creek and then Crenshaw Creek, you'll come to three waterfalls and the High Cascades of Crenshaw—a true thrill for the senses. While the

HIGH CASCADES ON CRENSHAW CREEK
Class: Sluice Height: 100+ ft Rating: Excellent

waterfalls are easily viewed at close range as you go, the High Cascades are mainly an auditory experience. For over half a mile, while dropping more than 100 feet, the waters of Crenshaw Creek slide, crash, and pound in a roar that echoes off the hillsides. What you see from the trail are mere glimpses of the glory of these falls. Above the cascades, you'll reach the last of the waterfalls and the turnaround point for the hike.

LOWER FALLS ON CRENSHAW
Class: Tiered Height: 10 ft Rating: Fair

Pinhoti Trail (cont.)

Getting to the Trailhead

From Milepost 8 on GA 52 west of Ellijay, take Gates Chapel Road 5.0 miles. Turn right on FS 241 and drive to the end of the road.

GPS Coordinates

N 34° 49.13' W 84° 33.84'

Hiking Directions

Begin Head for the end of the parking area, past the information board, and up Bear Creek Trail.

Mile 0.2 Pinhoti Trail enters from the left and shares the trail the rest of the route.

Mile 0.9 Pass the huge Gennett Poplar, Georgia's largest tulip poplar tree.

Mile 1.1 Turn right on Bear Creek Loop/Pinhoti Trail.

Mile 1.2 Turn left on woods road to remain on Bear Creek/Pinhoti Trail.

Mile 1.8 Turn right on Pinhoti Trail, continuing up and over the ridge.

Mile 3.2 Junction with Mountaintown Creek Trail. Turn left on Mountaintown Creek/Pinhoti Trail.

Mile 3.5 Ford the creek to a small campsite that marks the turnaround point for the Mountaintown Creek hike (p. 78). Heddy Branch and Crenshaw Creek converge here to form Mountaintown Creek. Continue up the trail along Crenshaw Creek.

Mile 3.8 Reach the small Lower Falls on Crenshaw Creek. It's down off the trail to the right.

Mile 4.8 The trail here becomes noticeably steeper. You should hear water crashing down to your right. For the next half-mile you'll climb along above the High Cascades.

Mile 5.7 Here you'll reach the first and second falls on Crenshaw Creek; one is right above the other. This is a good place to turn around as there are no more falls beyond this point. Return the way you came and enjoy the downhill—you deserve it.

Mile 11.4 Finish.

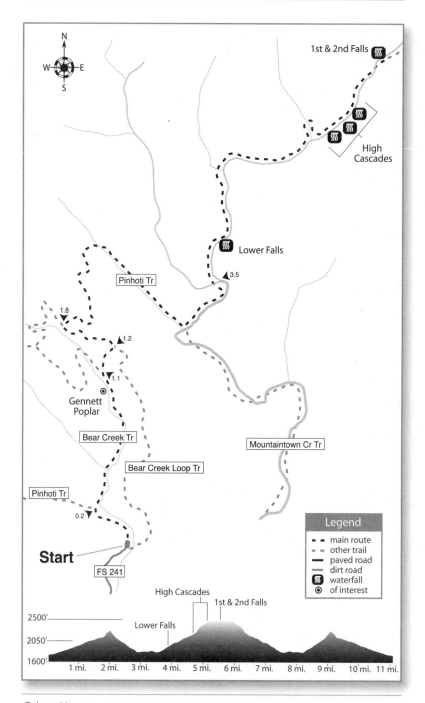

N
W E
S

1st & 2nd Falls

High Cascades

Lower Falls

3.5

Pinhoti Tr

1.8

1.2

1.1

Gennett Poplar

Bear Creek Tr

Bear Creek Loop Tr

Mountaintown Cr Tr

Pinhoti Tr

0.2

Start

FS 241

Legend
- - main route
- - other trail
— paved road
— dirt road
waterfall
of interest

High Cascades

1st & 2nd Falls

Lower Falls

2500'
2050'
1600'

1 mi. 2 mi. 3 mi. 4 mi. 5 mi. 6 mi. 7 mi. 8 mi. 9 mi. 10 mi. 11 mi.

Emery Creek Trail

Hike Distance:	6.4 miles
Type of Hike:	Out & Back
Number of Falls:	5
Hiking Time:	Half day
Dry Feet:	No
Start Elevation:	1,040 ft
Total Ascent:	1,000 ft
Land Manager:	USFS
Fee:	None

FIFTH FALLS ON EMERY CREEK
Class: Block Height: 15 feet Rating: Good

On this hike you'll travel the entire distance alongside Emery Creek. From the trailhead, you'll walk high above the creek for a short rocky stretch up to the confluence of Emery and Holly Creeks. It's a section popular with sun worshippers and creek swimmers, so you'll probably meet people walking along here as folks like to hang out in the rapids, pools, and small cascades. Once past Holly Creek, the first of many fords, you'll leave those folks behind.

Even with its frequent stream crossings, this hike is very pleasant. It climbs gently through a mixed hemlock and hardwood forest—cool on even the hottest of summer days—alongside the babbling, bubbling creek. Eventually the trail begins to climb more noticeably, and the creek quickens its pace accordingly. This is the sign that the falls are not far ahead. You'll cross the creek and turn on a short spur trail to the base of the first of them, a beauty dropping 40 feet. Skirt up and around it to see the second falls directly above, a wide 15-footer. Both of these have nice pools for splashing around in if you're so inclined.

Head back to the main trail and continue up, a bit more steeply now. It's not far to three more waterfalls, and soon you'll hear a roar through the rhododendron and see glimpses of whitewater and a definite falls below. Getting a closer look requires scrambling down the bank, but it's well worth the effort. These falls drop 15, 40, and 15 feet, and each has a nice plunge pool.

Emery Creek trail continues upward from here. An additional mile or so up the trail brings you to another 15-foot waterfall. However, after the power and beauty of the first five, it's hardly worth the extra effort and time required

FOURTH FALLS ON EMERY CREEK
Class: Tiered Height: 40 ft Rating: Excellent

to reach it. Unless you're serious about bagging or photographing waterfalls, it's best to turn back after viewing the fifth falls.

FIRST FALLS ON EMERY CREEK
Class: Tiered Height: 60 ft Rating: Excellent

Emery Creek Trail (cont.)

Getting to the Trailhead

Head west from Ellijay on GA 52. Just before the climb up Fort Mountain and beyond milepost 12, turn right on Conasauga Road. Go 1.2 miles to where the pavement ends. Continue straight onto FS 18 for another 5.0 miles to the trailhead parking lot on the right.

GPS Coordinates
N 34° 48.74' W 84° 39.13'

SECOND FALLS ON EMERY CREEK
Class: Block Height: 15 ft Rating: Good

Hiking Directions

Begin Head out of the back of the parking lot onto Emery Creek Trail which follows an old rocky roadbed.

Mile 0.3 Confluence of Emery and Holly Creek. Ford Holly and then Emery to continue.

Mile 1.3 The trail turns right onto a seeded roadbed.

Mile 1.4 Turn left off roadbed back onto trail. Do not ford the creek here.

Mile 2.2 Turn left onto a spur

Bonus Falls

HOLLY CREEK FALLS
Class: Segmented Height: 15 ft
Rating: Good

You'll pass this waterfall on your drive to the trailhead. It's easy to miss. From the intersection of FS 18 and FS 68, go 1.0 mile and pull off on the right. The falls is found at the bottom of a steep hill through some big hemlocks.

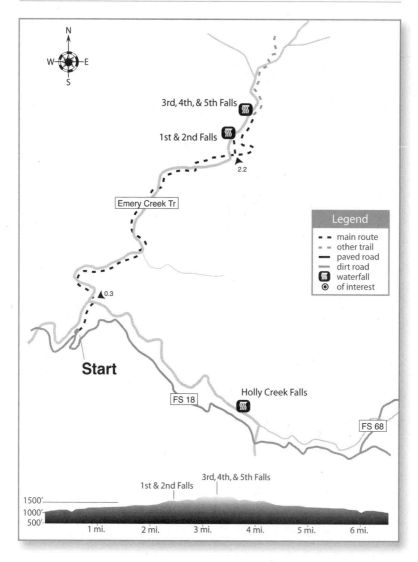

1st & 2nd Falls

3rd, 4th, & 5th Falls

Emery Creek Tr

▲2.2

Emery Creek Tr

▲0.3

Start

FS 18

Holly Creek Falls

FS 68

Legend

- – – main route
- – – other trail
- —— paved road
- —— dirt road
- 〰 waterfall
- ◉ of interest

1st & 2nd Falls

3rd, 4th, & 5th Falls

1500'
1000'
500'

1 mi. 2 mi. 3 mi. 4 mi. 5 mi. 6 mi.

trail signposted "To Emery Creek Falls."

Mile 2.3 Base of first falls, a 60-footer with a nice pool at the bottom. There is a second falls above this one. After viewing, return to the main trail and turn left up the mountain.

Mile 3.2 Here you'll find the third, fourth, and fifth falls, with the middle one the highest at 40 feet. This is a good place to turn around.

Mile 6.4 Finish.

Gahutti–Cool Springs Loop

Hike Distance:	5.2 miles
Type of Hike:	Loop
Number of Falls:	4+
Hiking Time:	Half day
Dry Feet:	Yes
Start Elevation:	2,583 ft
Total Ascent:	1,554 ft
Land Manager:	State Park
Fee:	$3

First Falls on Mill Creek
Class: Tiered Height: 50 ft Rating: Good

ort Mountain sits high above Georgia's Great Valley and marks the western edge of the southern Blue Ridge. The overlooks there offer commanding views, and on a clear day you can see Lookout Mountain far to the west. On the very top is an ancient stone wall of unknown origin, some 850 feet in length. There are several theories as to how it got here. The most plausible one is that it was built by the Woodland Indians around 500 BC. The most romantic is that it was built by a Welsh prince 500 years ago. And the most boring is that it is not a wall at all, but the result of natural weathering of a stone outcrop. However it got there, it's the "fort" in Fort Mountain. Today, the top of the mountain and the area surrounding it are protected for our enjoyment as Fort Mountain State Park.

The Park itself boasts cabins, camping, swimming, and picnicking facilities second to none. It also has one of the best trail networks of any state park in Georgia, accommodating hikers, mountain bikers, and horseback riders alike. Even better, on these trails you can expect to find several very nice waterfalls.

Once in the Park, be sure to stop by the ranger station and obtain a free hiking permit. The rangers like to know where you're headed. If you get into any difficulty they can help you out; they can also inform you of any trail hazards or closures. Expect to pay a hefty fine if you forgo the permit and are caught without one.

This hike first follows the Gahutti Backcountry Trail and then the Cool Springs Loop Trail to a series of waterfalls on Mill Creek. If it has recently rained, you'll see several additional falls on the small feeder streams.

SECOND FALLS ON MILL CREEK (UPPER)
Class: Tiered Height: 50 ft Rating: Good

All of them fall into the boulder-strewn stairstep category, dropping many feet over a significant distance, so it's almost impossible to see an entire waterfall at once. No matter—with their green, moss-covered rocks and sparkling clear, splashing water they'll give you just the inspiration you'll need for the climb back up to the top of the mountain to end the hike.

SECOND FALLS ON MILL CREEK (LOWER)
Class: Tiered Height: 50 ft Rating: Good

Gahutti-Cool Springs Loop (cont.)

Getting to the Trailhead

Fort Mountain State Park is located on GA 52 between Chatsworth and Ellijay. This route starts at the Cool Springs Overlook Parking Lot.

GPS Coordinates
N 34° 46.73' W 84° 42.32'

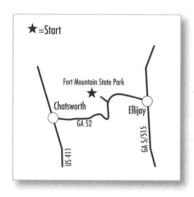

★ =Start

Fort Mountain State Park
★
Chatsworth
Ellijay
GA 52
US 411
GA 5/515

Hiking Directions

Begin Walk east on the Gahutti Trail, away from the overlook.

Mile 1.5 Cross the small stream and at campsite #1, turn left.

Mile 1.6 Cross the bridge and turn left onto trail #301.

Mile 2.4 After passing several small feeder stream falls you'll again reach Mill Creek. There is a 20-foot broken rock jumble falls here as well. The best view is from the trail.

Mile 2.8 Sluices and cascades along this stretch are more easily heard than seen. Look for a 20-foot-high stairstep waterfall that drops over a 50-foot distance.

Mile 2.9 Switchbacks lead down past a second stairstep falls which drops another 60 feet over a series of sluices and mossy rock tiers—very impressive.

Mile 3.3 Turn left at the #5 checkpoint and head steeply uphill.

Mile 3.7 Turn left off the woods road to stay on trail #301.

Mile 4.3 A series of steep, rocky switchbacks brings you to checkpoint #4. Turn left on trail #302.

Mile 5.0 Turn left Gahutti Trail.

Mile 5.1 Cool Springs Observation Platform. Enjoy the view.

Mile 5.2 Finish.

Second Falls on Mill Creek (middle)
Class: Tiered Height: 50 ft Rating: Good

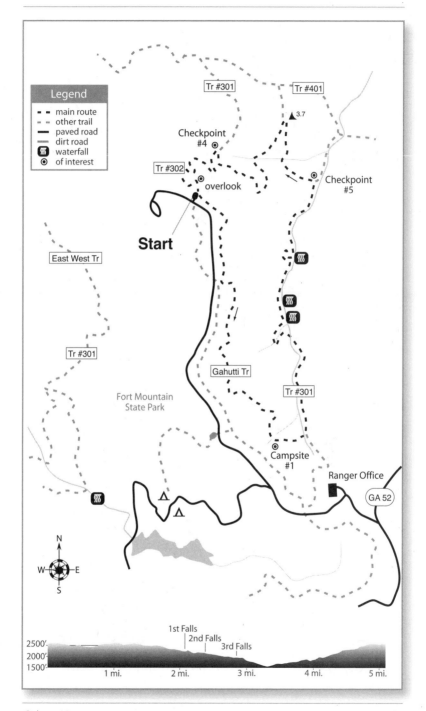

Legend
- - main route
- - other trail
— paved road
— dirt road
waterfall
of interest

Tr #301

Tr #401

▲3.7

Checkpoint #4

Tr #302

overlook

Checkpoint #5

Start

East West Tr

Tr #301

Gahutti Tr

Tr #301

Fort Mountain
State Park

Campsite #1

Ranger Office

GA 52

N
W — E
S

1st Falls
2nd Falls
3rd Falls

2500'
2000'
1500'

1 mi.   2 mi.   3 mi.   4 mi.   5 mi.

Gold Mine Creek Falls

Hike Distance:	4 miles
Type of Hike:	Lollipop
Number of Falls:	2
Hiking Time:	Half day
Dry Feet:	Yes
Start Elevation:	2,405 ft
Total Ascent:	1,000 ft
Land Manager:	State Park
Fee:	$3

LOWER GOLD MINE CREEK FALLS
Class: Tiered Height: 400 ft Rating: Good

Talc mining on Fort Mountain began around 1900. For a while it was the state's leading source of the mineral. Talc from Georgia was used to make paper, plastics, pharmaceuticals, and ceramics. You might be most familiar with it as a major ingredient in talcum powder.

On this hike you'll pass at least four abandoned talc mines. They're nothing fancy; they are bored into the side of the mountain, with openings that resemble cave entrances. Near the entrances, remnants of past work remain—old sheds, loose metal, and the like. Be careful around these mines. Most have been barricaded to keep folks out, but you know how well that works; on some, parts of the barricade have been removed. Walk up near the entrance and take a peek in, but going beyond that is just plain dangerous. Take this hike on a cold, damp day and you might see smoke-like steam puffing out of vent holes in the sides of the mountain.

So why isn't the creek that forms the waterfall on this hike called Talc Mine Creek? Well, there was once a gold mine here, and it predated the talc mines. The stream became Gold Mine Creek before talc was discovered. The old gold mine is located just above the lake on the upper portion of the creek; you will not pass it on this hike.

This is one of those routes that starts high, descends, and then ends with an uphill pull. In this case, both the uphill and the downhill are a real challenge. For just over half a mile both going and coming, you'll tackle an extremely steep hill. It's not rocky or technical, just steep. It's hard on the knees going down and on the achilles tendon coming back up. Trailbuilders took advantage of a preexisting powerline cut when they constructed the trail, even though the straight uphill and straight down that works for powerlines is the opposite of hiker-friendly. Wouldn't it be great if you could "transmit" yourself over this portion of trail?

Gold Mine Creek Falls is a very high waterfall. It starts out plummeting over a cliff and ends by crashing down through a long jumble of boulders. From the bottom you can barely see the water dropping over the cliff high above. Viewed from the top, it just disappears over the lip as you gaze at the town of Chatsworth far below.

If the conditions are right (after a period of wet weather), you'll see another waterfall on this hike. Beyond the bottom of Gold Mine Creek and past three talc mines is a very small falls that slithers its way down a vertical rock face. It's just off the trail and right beside the entrance to a mine, but be forewarned—a healthy stand of poison ivy guards the base.

CLIFF FACE WATERFALL
Class: Tiered   Height: 40 ft   Rating: Good

Gold Mine Creek Falls (cont.)

Getting to the Trailhead

Fort Mountain State Park is located on GA 52 between Chatsworth and Ellijay. This route starts just beyond the dam on the Big Rock Nature Trail.

GPS Coordinates
N 34° 45.43′ W 84° 42.66′

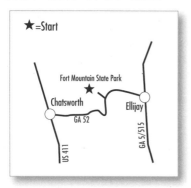

Hiking Directions

Begin Head down the left fork of the Big Rock Nature Trail.

Mile 0.2 Turn left onto the Gahutti Trail that heads along the rim of the mountain.

Mile 0.5 Gahutti Trail veers left here. Go straight onto the very short spur trail out to the powerline cut and turn right on East West Trail #301. The next half-mile is a very steep downhill.

Mile 0.8 Pass the first of several abandoned talc mine shafts.

Mile 1.1 Drop down onto a dirt roadbed and turn right. Almost immediately trail #301 turns off to the left. Continue straight onto trail #407.

Mile 1.5 Here is the base of lower Gold Mine Creek Falls.

Mile 1.9 You'll pass three more mine shafts and then reach a waterfall on a cliff face, guarded closely by poison ivy. This is a good place to turn around. Retrace your route back to Big Rock Nature Trail, being sure to give yourself plenty of time for the very steep uphill on the return.

Mile 3.6 Cross a footbridge and turn left to remain on the Gahutti Trail as it merges with Big Rock Nature Trail.

Mile 3.8 Here is the upper portion of Gold Mine Creek Falls. Do not cross the creek, but turn right on Big Rock Nature Trail.

Mile 4.0 Walk up below the dam to finish.

UPPER GOLD MINE CREEK FALLS
Class: Tiered Height: 40 ft Rating: Good

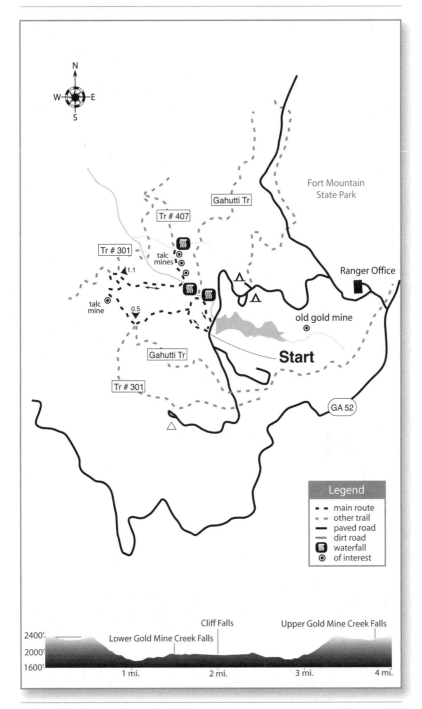

N
W • E
S

Fort Mountain
State Park

Gahutti Tr

Tr # 407

Tr # 301

talc
mines

1.1

talc
mine

0.5

Ranger Office

old gold mine

Start

Gahutti Tr

Tr # 301

GA 52

Legend

- - main route
- - - other trail
—— paved road
—— dirt road
🏞 waterfall
⊙ of interest

Cliff Falls

Upper Gold Mine Creek Falls

Lower Gold Mine Creek Falls

2400'
2000'
1600'

1 mi.   2 mi.   3 mi.   4 mi.

Western Blue Ridge

Second Falls on Little Rock Creek

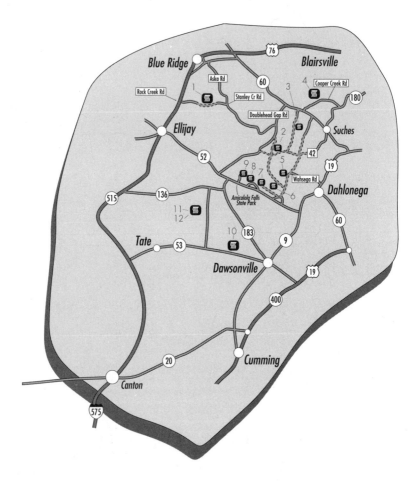

Take a pencil and draw a line roughly following GA 60 from Suches to Blue Ridge. Now draw another line along GA 53 from Dawsonville to Tate. Sandwiched in between is the eastern section of north Georgia's western Blue Ridge Mountains. Good thing we put it in a sandwich because that's a mouthful! To simplify things, we'll just call it the Western Blue Ridge. It's a great place to go looking for waterfalls. High mountains here send water cascading off to the west and eventually into the Gulf of Mexico, via either the Tennessee and Mississippi River systems or the Alabama River system. You'll find Georgia's highest and second-highest waterfalls here—Amicalola at 729 feet and Cochrans at 600 feet are also the third- and fifth-highest waterfalls east of the Mississippi.

Not only are there beautiful waterfalls here, there's great hiking as well. Several of Georgia's long-distance trails begin or terminate here. Most famous of all is the Appalachian National Scenic Trail, known simply to most as the Appalachian Trail or AT. Its southern terminus is atop Springer Mountain, just above Amicalola Falls State Park. You can hike along a portion of it on the Three Forks hike (p. 108). On that very hike you'll also follow two other of Georgia's long-distance trails, Benton MacKaye and Duncan Ridge. Benton MacKaye Trail travels

north to the Great Smoky Mountains in Tennessee and North Carolina for a total of 288 miles, and Duncan Ridge Trail goes west for a more modest but still demanding 35 miles. Other trails in the region, while not as long, provide excellent opportunities for a day's outing. The ones listed in this book also head off in the direction of a waterfall or two.

Be sure to give yourself plenty of time for each of these hikes, including the drive to and from the trailhead. While some are just off the highway, others require negotiating twisty, bumpy gravel mountain roads.

UPPER EAST FORK OF JONES CREEK

Stanley Gap Loop

Hike Distance:	4.6 miles
Type of Hike:	Loop
Number of Falls:	2
Hiking Time:	2 hours
Dry Feet:	Maybe
Start Elevation:	2,068 ft
Total Ascent:	1,200 ft
Land Manager:	USFS
Fee:	None

FALL BRANCH FALLS
Class: Tiered Height: 60 ft Rating: Good

Some waterfall purists might just decide to walk the short distance upstream on each of these creeks to their respective falls and call it a day—bag two falls and head off in search for more. But those who enjoy a good walk in the woods will elect the loop hike instead. Sure, you'll do a bit more climbing and it'll take a little longer, but after the time you spent getting here in the car, a good leg-stretcher is usually just what the doctor ordered.

People have been building vacation homes on privately owned mountain land between Ellijay and Blue Ridge for generations. Years ago such a home was just a small cabin in the woods, a place to get away from the hubbub of cities like Atlanta and the steamy climate of Florida and chill out during the cooler mountain summers. But not too many years back, something changed in what folks think of as a cabin. Look across the hillsides now and you'll see not cabins, which typically blend into the landscape, but two-story, three-story, and larger structures sprouting like so many weeds in what was once a smooth expanse of green mountainside. As private land has become more scarce, entire gated communities have sprung up on impossibly steep terrain. Property adjacent to national forest, overlooking cliffs, or right on top of waterfalls goes for big bucks.

All this stares you right in the face when you take the short stroll up to Fall Branch Falls. On one side of the stream is the Chattahoochee National Forest—it's green, it's quiet, it's pretty. On the other side is development—complete with keep out signs and barbed wire fences. At the time of this writing, there were for sale signs a mere six feet from the stream bank, right at the base of the waterfall.

Imagine you can see the future. You walk up to view the falls. From the observation platform at the bottom, you look up and see the falls in all its glory. Shift your eyes to the right a few feet, and there's someone eating breakfast on their deck. Doesn't that make you want to build another "cabin" in woods?

The great thing about this hike is that by continuing up the mountain and around the loop, you can get away from all that, and rather quickly. Benton Mackaye Trail leads you right on up to the spine of Rich Mountain, where you'll take Stanley Gap Trail back down to the gap. Next, a forest road hike will take you up to the very edge of the Rich Mountain Wilderness, where no development of any kind will ever happen. Then you're off in search of another waterfall, this one on the cool waters of Stanley Creek, and just a bit more remote.

STANLEY CREEK FALLS
Class: Tiered Height: 8 ft Rating: Fair

Stanley Gap Loop (cont.)

Getting to the Trailhead

From GA 515 in Blue Ridge, take Windy Ridge Road 0.1 mile south, turn left on East 1st Street, go 0.1 mile and turn right on Aska Road. Drive 7.2 miles and turn right on Stanley Gap Road. Go another 3.0 miles to the Fall Branch Falls trailhead on the right.

GPS Coordinates

N 34° 47.06' W 84° 18.12'

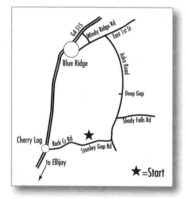

★ =Start

Hiking Directions

Begin From the trailhead, walk up the left side of Fall Creek. The right side is private land.

Mile 0.2 A side trail on the right leads to the base of Fall Creek Falls and a viewing platform. After viewing the falls from below, continue up the trail as it climbs beside the falls. Pay close attention here as you'll turn left off this trail and onto the continuation of the Benton Mackaye Trail just before reaching the top.

Mile 1.1 Turn left on Stanley Gap Trail.

Mile 1.8 Pass Stanley Gap trailhead parking lot. Turn right on the entrance road to the lot and walk down to Stanley Gap Road where you'll turn right.

Mile 1.9 Turn left past the gate on FS 338.

Mile 2.8 At the gap, turn left on Stanley Creek Trail. There is no trail sign here but the path is well defined. Head down alongside the boundary to the Rich Mountain Wilderness.

Mile 3.3 A trail exits to the right and crosses a bridge over Stanley Creek. Continue straight down the left side of the creek.

Mile 3.5 You'll have to ford the creek here. If you're good at rockhopping, you may be able to keep your feet dry.

Mile 4.0 Here you'll pass the only notable waterfall on this section of Stanley Creek. It's below the trail to the right.

Mile 4.1 Turn right here and walk down Stanley Creek Road.

Mile 4.6 Finish.

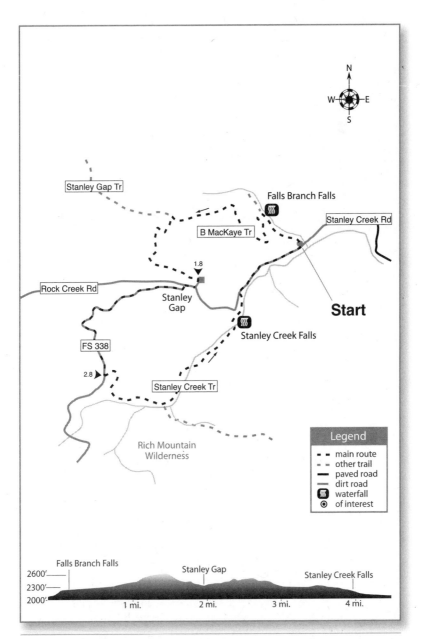

Stanley Gap Tr

Falls Branch Falls

B MacKaye Tr

Stanley Creek Rd

1.8

Rock Creek Rd

Stanley
Gap

Start

Stanley Creek Falls

FS 338

2.8

Stanley Creek Tr

Rich Mountain
Wilderness

Legend
- - main route
- - other trail
— paved road
— dirt road
▓ waterfall
◉ of interest

Falls Branch Falls
Stanley Gap
Stanley Creek Falls

2600'
2300'
2000'

1 mi.   2 mi.   3 mi.   4 mi.

Three Forks West

Hike Distance:	2.7 miles
Type of Hike:	Out & Back
Number of Falls:	3
Hiking Time:	2 hours
Dry Feet:	Yes
Start Elevation:	2,550 ft
Total Ascent:	800 ft
Land Manager:	USFS
Fee:	None

FIRST FALLS ON LONG CREEK
Class: Fan Height: 25 ft Rating: Good

Sometimes people come up with what they think is an original-sounding name and just go with it. That's why we get hiking store names like *The Happy Hiker* and *Footsloggers* or bike shop names like *Chain Reaction* and *Biketown*. If only these folks would do a little research, they'd see there are any number of *Happy Hikers*, *Footsloggers*, *Chain Reactions*, and *Biketowns* scattered around the globe. Place names are no different. In north Georgia there are at least two *Three Forks*. This is the westernmost one where Chester Fork, Stover Creek, and Long Creek meet to form Noontootla Creek. It's also where three separate long-distance foot trails converge. The Appalachian Trail and Benton Mackaye Trail share the same tread for a while, and out near the third waterfall is the western terminus of Duncan Ridge Trail. So, Three Forks is a doubly good name.

It's a treat to hike to a series of waterfalls right on the AT. That doesn't happen anywhere else in north Georgia; for the most part the AT clings to the ridgetops. Here you'll follow the track of an old woods road through stands of huge hemlock and mixed hardwoods as you gradually climb alongside Long Creek. If you're here between late March and the end of May, chances are you'll run into some "thru-hikers." These are folks attempting to hike the entire AT—over 2,000 miles from Georgia to Maine—in one straight shot. Many of these northbounders will have started from the shelter atop Springer Mountain only that morning, and it will be their first full day on the trail. Expect them to be in high spirits, optimistic, and eager to go. Be sure to wish them good luck on their journey.

Of the three falls along this route, the third is the easiest to get to, as a marked trail takes you

THIRD FALLS ON LONG CREEK
Class: Tiered Height: 60 ft Rating: Excellent

directly to it. The other two are somewhat more hidden, but you shouldn't have any trouble identifying the goatpaths that lead to them. You'll find small, refreshing plunge pools at the bottom of some remarkable drops. Take time to enjoy each one.

With Noontootla Falls just down the road and Little Rock Creek Falls in the next watershed just over the ridge, consider making this hike part of a Three Forks–Little Rock Creek–Sea Creek Tour (p. 282).

SECOND FALLS ON LONG CREEK
Class: Tiered Height: 60+ ft Rating: Excellent

Three Forks West (cont.)

Getting to the Trailhead

From the junction of Highway 515 and GA 60 just north of Blue Ridge, drive 13 miles on GA 60 and turn right on Doublehead Gap Road. Continue another 5.8 miles and turn left on FS 58. From here it is 3.2 miles to Noontootla Falls and 5.6 miles to Three Forks. You'll find the trailhead where the AT crosses the road.

GPS Coordinates

N 34° 39.80' W 84° 11.04'

Hiking Directions

Begin From the trailhead, hike north on the Appalachian Trail. If you went south by mistake, you'd immediately cross a footbridge over the creek.

Mile 0.7 A goatpath leads to the first falls on Long Creek, a 25-foot-high fan with a small pool at the bottom. You should be able to hear it down in the rhodo thicket and then just follow the noise.

Mile 1.0 Just before you reach this point you can see and hear the second falls through the jumble of rhododendron. Look for a goatpath heading off in that direction. It leads to the top of the waterfall. This 60-footer starts with a slide, then enters a choked sluice before a final 35-foot drop which splits through a cleft in the rock.

Mile 1.2 Junction of four trails. Take Long Creek Falls Trail, farthest to the left.

Bonus Falls

NOONTOOTLA FALLS
Class: Tiered Height: 75 ft
Rating: Excellent

Noontootla Falls is located 2.4 miles north of Three Forks on FS 58, or 3.2 miles from the northern end of FS 58. To get to the main drop from the road, walk 0.1 mile up the left side of Noontootla Creek alongside the lower sluices and tiers of the waterfall.

Mile 1.3 Long Creek Falls, a three-tiered drop of 60 feet. It's not too difficult to skirt up the right side to see the top tiers. Return from here the way you came.

Mile 2.6 Finish.

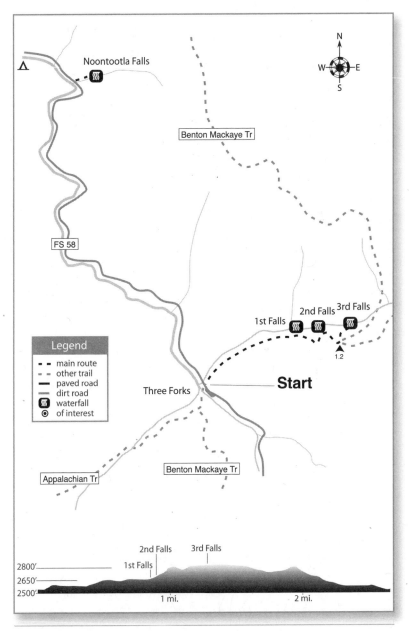

Little Rock Creek Falls

Hike Distance:	1.2 miles
Type of Hike:	Out & Back
Number of Falls:	2
Hiking Time:	1 hour
Dry Feet:	Yes
Start Elevation:	2,142 ft
Total Ascent:	400 ft
Land Manager:	USFS
Fee:	None

SECOND FALLS ON LITTLE ROCK CREEK
Class: Horsetail Height: 50 ft Rating: Excellent

Wildflowers are almost as much fun to spot as waterfalls. Hiking in north Georgia in the spring, summer, and early fall, you get to see both. When a creek comes crashing down over the side of a mountain, typically the water flies in all directions. Often a fine mist fills the air in a small radius around the waterfall. This constantly moist environment creates just the right conditions for all manner of special plants and animals. Take a second look at that quivering white mass on the rock beside the falls. It might be a clump of flowering mountain lettuce which somehow found a foothold in a tiny crevice. In late April, look for foam flowers to be blooming all around the base of the second falls on Little Rock Creek. The draft created by the falls causes the blooms to constantly wave back and forth as they shimmer with the moisture beaded on their petals. It's a sight to see—and it certainly adds to the pleasure of viewing this waterfall.

It's just a short, easy-to-moderate hike up to the first and second falls on Little Rock Creek. Once you're out of your car you'll notice two distinct footpaths heading up the left side of the creek. Most folks take the one closest to the stream because it's a little more worn down than the other. Resist this urge and take the higher path; it will lead you up and around the thick vegetation and eventually provide much better footing. Neither of these trails is marked.

You'll climb steadily above the creek for a short way and then drop back down to it. Be sure to take care in the few slippery places. All along the way, cascades and rapids crash. Before long you'll reach the first falls of any size, a 10-foot double drop with a pretty pool at the bottom. Continuing on, you'll reach the main attraction

of this hike right at the head of a mini-gorge. It's shaped like three sides of a bowl with the waterfall pouring over the cliff, right in the middle. The falls itself is a classic horsetail that crashes down on rocks, springs out, and makes a dogleg twist before falling into a small pool. With hardly a moment to rest, the water quickly sluices down a 20-foot waterslide. It's exciting just to look at it.

Expect to see a good number of tall hemlocks all around the bowl and on the hike in. These mighty trees stand like brave sentinels guarding the creek while thick green rhododendron bushes crowd to the edges below. What a place! At any moment you might expect to see some fantastical green, gnome-like creature come jumping out from behind a rock.

It shouldn't take you too long to see all there is to see here, so consider making this hike part of the Three Forks—Little Rock Creek—Sea Creek Tour (p. 282). The scenic drive along the various forest roads alone would make it worth the trip.

FIRST FALLS ON LITTLE ROCK CREEK
Class: Tiered Height: 10 ft Rating: Fair

Little Rock Creek Falls (cont.)

Getting to the Trailhead

From the junction of Highway 515 and GA 60 just north of Blue Ridge, drive 17.0 miles on GA 60 and turn right on Rock Creek Road. Continue another 3.3 miles and park at the pullout on either side of the bridge crossing Little Rock Creek.

GPS Coordinates

N 34° 42.99′ W 84° 09.10

Bonus Falls

ROCK CREEK FALLS
Class: Tiered Height: 15 ft Rating: Fair

You'll find this falls just off FS 69 (Rock Creek Road), directly below the man-made 40-foot waterfall formed by the dam at Rock Creek Lake. To get there, continue another 3.6 miles beyond the trailhead to Little Rock Creek Falls. You'll pass right by here should you decide to drive the Three Forks West–Little Rock Creek Falls–Sea Creek Falls Tour on p. 282.

Hiking Directions

Begin Walk up the well-defined but unmarked trail on the left, facing upstream on the creek. You'll see two paths; be sure to take the upper trail.

Mile 0.4 Here is the first falls, a small, double-tiered 10-footer.

Mile 0.6 Second falls. This is a much larger drop—a classic 50-foot horsetail into a small pool, followed by a 20-foot waterslide. Return from here the way you came.

Mile 1.2 Finish.

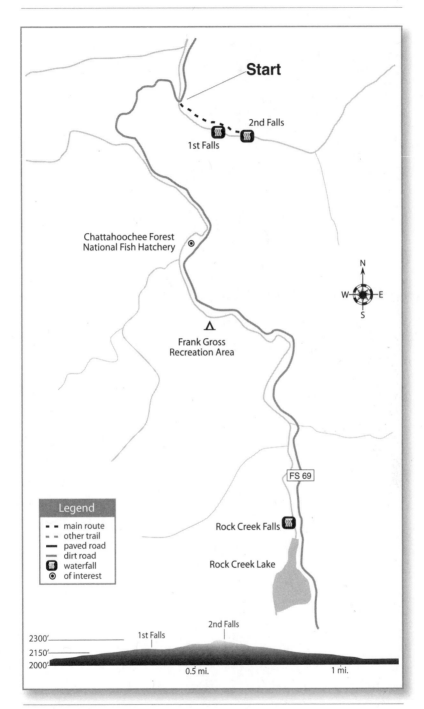

Start

2nd Falls

1st Falls

Chattahoochee Forest
National Fish Hatchery

Frank Gross
Recreation Area

N
W—E
S

FS 69

Rock Creek Falls

Rock Creek Lake

Legend
- - main route
- - other trail
— paved road
— dirt road
🌊 waterfall
⊙ of interest

2300'
2150'
2000'

1st Falls

2nd Falls

0.5 mi.

1 mi.

Sea Creek Falls

Hike Distance:	0.7 miles
Type of Hike:	Out & Back
Number of Falls:	1
Hiking Time:	1 hour
Dry Feet:	Maybe
Start Elevation:	2,239 ft
Total Ascent:	100 ft
Land Manager:	USFS
Fee:	None

SEA CREEK FALLS
Class: Tiered Height: 40 ft Rating: Excellent

This book has long hikes, difficult hikes, short hikes, and easy hikes, with a lot in between. For those who want something short *and* easy, this hike meets both criteria.

Sea Creek Falls has three distinct tiers, each sliding into the next. The bottom drop carves into a cliff, forming what looks like a cave mouth, open wide and swallowing the whole creek before spitting it out to the side. To keep your feet dry, walk right up to the falls on an old roadbed, and you can see it pretty well from where you stand. For the best view, though, you'll have to step into the creek, wade the shallow water across the gravel streambed, and take a look from the other side.

Getting to the Trailhead

From the junction of Highway 515 and GA 60 just north of Blue Ridge, drive 18.0 miles on GA 60 and turn left on Cooper Creek Road at Cooper Creek Store. Continue 3.0 miles and turn left on FS 264. It's another 0.2 mile to the trailhead, just before the creek ford.

GPS Coordinates
N 34° 46.05′ W 84° 05.78′

Hiking Directions

Begin From the trailhead, walk up the old roadbed to the left of the creek. Do not ford the creek— not yet.

Mile 0.3 Sea Creek Falls. Cross the creek, enjoy the view, then return the way you came.

Mile 0.7 Finish.

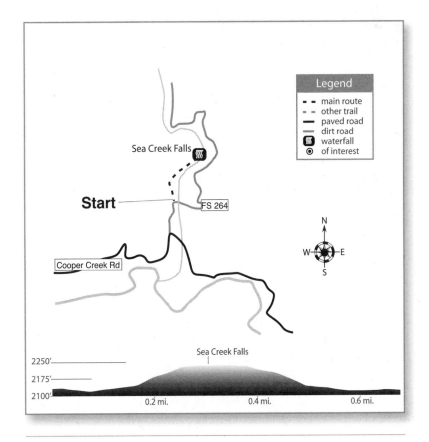

Black Falls of the Etowah

Hike Distance:	1 mile
Type of Hike:	Loop
Number of Falls:	2
Hiking Time:	1 hour
Dry Feet:	No
Start Elevation:	1,820 ft
Total Ascent:	250 ft
Land Manager:	US Army
Fee:	None

BLACK FALLS OF THE ETOWAH
Class: Tiered Height: 60 ft Rating: Excellent

BOOM. BANG. RATA-TAT-TAT. FWHUMP, FWHUMP, FWHUMP.
Sounds like you've just entered a war zone. Actually, you're hiking
down to see the Black Falls of the Etowah River. The trail just happens
to be on the grounds of U.S. Army Camp Frank D. Merrill, where the
5th Army Training Battalion—Army Rangers—undergoes its mountain
training. Those noises you hear are heavy artillery, machine guns, and
helicopters flying about. They are a ways off (otherwise you would not
be allowed here), but they sound close enough. What an exciting place
to go for a hike!

What does a soldier do here? He trains day and night working
alone and with a platoon, at the base and on cross-country treks over
the mountains. He might ambush a vehicle, raid a mortar site, cross a
wild river, or scale a mountain cliff. Sometimes he'll make an air assault
to a tiny landing zone on the side of a steep mountain or march 10
miles over the top of the ridges behind the camp, his stamina stressed
to the max. At any time he may be called on to lead exhausted, hungry

soldiers on yet another mission.

After this description, you must be wondering, is it safe to hike here? Is it even allowed? The answer to both is yes, but with caveats. First, you must be absolutely certain to stop at the guard house by the camp's main entrance and check to be sure no maneuvers are going on in the vicinity of the falls. Let the guard know you'd like to walk down and see the waterfalls. Unless he tells you otherwise, you should be good to go.

Second, do not under any circumstances climb on or tamper with any of the equipment on the activity field below the falls, the rappelling cliff, or the climbing wall. Finally, don't do anything else that would jeopardize the willingness of the Army to let the general public visit this special place.

All that said, this is a really neat hike. Not only do you get to see two rather large waterfalls, but you get to see some of where the Rangers train. All kinds of things are set up to keep these folks battle-ready. In addition to the sheer cliff for rappelling down and the wooden tower for climbing up, there are various types of obstacle courses. A removable gate allows the river to be temporarily dammed, and right above the lower falls is a high rope bridge. You wouldn't want to fall off that thing.

The falls themselves are both rated excellent. Black Falls drops around 60 feet in a tiered staircase. A small footbridge at the bottom gives you an excellent view. The lower falls, which you'll see first, drops in two distinct tiers with a short stretch of water in between. It falls about 45 feet in all and has a large plunge pool at the bottom.

There you have it—a short, sweet hike that ends with a bang.

LOWER FALLS
Class: Tiered   Height: 45 ft   Rating: Excellent

Black Falls of the Etowah (cont.)

Getting to the Trailhead

From Dahlonega, take U.S.19B north out of town for 2.0 miles. Turn left on Wahsega Road and drive another 9.5 miles to U.S. Army Camp Frank D. Merrill and turn left on FS 28. Go 0.4 mile and park at the trailhead immediately beyond S. Sergent R. Portfollo Road.

GPS Coordinates
N 34° 37.28' W 84° 06.22'

Hiking Directions

Begin Just to the left of S. Sergent R. Portfollo Road is a trail/old road heading down into the woods. Take this down the hill.

Mile 0.2 Turn left at the bottom of the hill and head downstream alongside the river.

Mile 0.3 There is a river ford here well above the first waterfall. You can ford the river now and view the falls from the opposite shore, or head down to the falls

and view from this side first. Stay on this side if you want to keep your feet dry, but the view is better from the other side. Either way, once you've seen the falls, head back upstream along either side of the river.

Mile 0.7 Walk across the military training field and past the rappelling cliff to the base of Black Falls. Again, stay off any training equipment. The bridge at the base of the falls offers the best view. When you've seen enough, head up the hill on the road between the rappelling cliff and the climbing tower.

Mile 1.0 Finish.

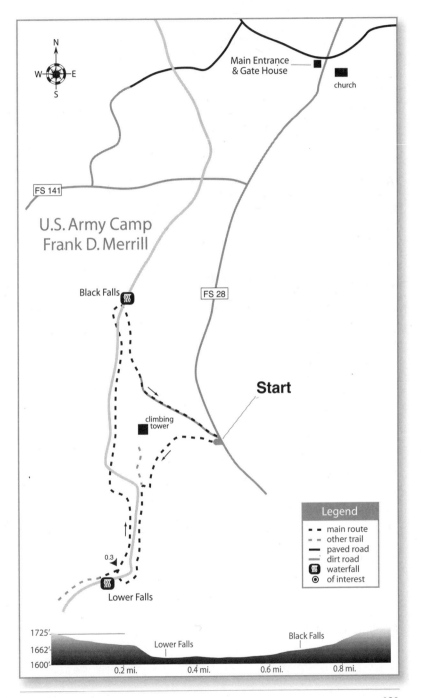

N
W—E
S

Main Entrance
& Gate House

church

FS 141

U.S. Army Camp
Frank D. Merrill

Black Falls

FS 28

Start

climbing
tower

Legend
- - main route
- - other trail
— paved road
— dirt road
waterfall
of interest

0.3

Lower Falls

1725'
1662'
1600'

Lower Falls

Black Falls

0.2 mi.   0.4 mi.   0.6 mi.   0.8 mi.

Forks of Jones Creek

Hike Distance:	1 mile
Type of Hike:	Out & Back
Number of Falls:	4
Hiking Time:	1 hour
Dry Feet:	Maybe
Total Ascent:	50 ft
Land Manager:	USFS
Fee:	None

FALLS BRANCH FALLS
Class: Triple Horsetail Height: 15 ft Rating: Fair

Two short hikes for the price of one—that's what you get at Forks of Jones Creek. It's a good thing, too, as the drive into this area is on a dusty and bumpy gravel forest road, making the distance seem longer than the actual number of miles covered.

Starting high on the slopes of Springer Mountain, the southern terminus of the Appalachian Trail, Jones Creek springs out of the ground and heads down the mountain, gaining in size and branching and forking as it goes. As you wade out into the sizable stream to begin your walk, it's hard to believe hikers up on the AT (spending what could be their first or last night on the trail) get their drinking water from a tiny spring—and that spring is the head of the same creek you're sloshing through.

Like any stream in the mountains, Jones Creek has many tributaries. It's on two of these tributaries that the waterfalls for these two hikes are located. First up and the farthest to drive to is Falls Branch, a cold, clear stream that drops down off Ball Mountain, the peak adjacent to Springer. You'll start right where Falls Branch enters Jones Creek and walk upstream from there. It's only a short distance, and Falls Branch Falls, though only 15 feet high, is quite nice. Unless it's a raging torrent the day you visit, expect to see three horsetails plunging over a boulder face. And if it *is* a raging torrent, take care on that creek ford.

Now drive back down the road about a half-mile to the Upper East Fork, the next branch that flows into Jones Creek. Here, take another short walk downstream, this time to not just one but three waterfalls. If you had your car window open on the drive in, you may have heard them crashing through the rhododendron thickets below the road. One follows right behind another as they spread out over a 0.1-mile stretch of the stream. First look for a 10-foot-high, 30-foot-long waterslide. This is fol-

lowed by a stairstep tier of 25 feet, and finally it all crashes to an end with a 20-foot double stairstep drop. Each alone is rated just fair, but take them all together, and they're quite impressive.

MIDDLE FALLS UPPER EAST FORK OF JONES CREEK
Class: Tiered Height: 25 ft Rating: Fair

Forks of Jones Creek (cont.)

Getting to Trailhead #1

From Nimblewill Baptist Church on Nimblewill Road east of Dahlonega via GA 52, drive 2.2 miles on FS 28-2. Turn left on FS 77 and drive 1.3 miles to turn left on FS 77-A. Continue another 1.8 miles to a campground info board where you'll turn right onto FS 877. Continue 0.8 mile and park just before the first ford or between the first and second fords, depending on the depth of creek or the clearance of your car. **Caution:** Possible creek ford.

GPS Coordinates
N 34° 36.51' W 84° 09.52'

Getting to Trailhead #2

From Trailhead #1, backtrack 0.4 mile and park on the shoulder of the road where the Upper East Fork of Jones Creek passes underneath.

GPS Coordinates
N 34° 36.18' W 84° 08.10'

Hiking Directions #1

Begin Depending on where you parked, either wade the creek and walk a short distance before turning right up past a T-bar and onto the trail, or just walk up past the T-bar that marks the end of the old roadbed trail. The trail is not marked but it's well used. You might also notice the goatpath that leads up the other side of the creek. You can go that way, but this is a much better route.

Mile 0.25 The waterfall is down on your right. The trail continues, but you should turn back here and return the way you came.

Mile 0.5 Finish.

Hiking Directions #2

Begin Enter the woods about 30 feet to the left of the creek and follow the goatpath that highsides the left shore heading downstream. The falls are just ahead.

Mile 0.25 All three waterfalls, one right after the other, are between mile 0.1 and 0.2. The first is a 10-foot-high, 30-foot-long waterslide. The second is a 25-foot tiered stairstep, and the third is a 20-foot double tier. After the third waterfall, turn back and retrace your steps to the start.

Mile 0.5 Finish.

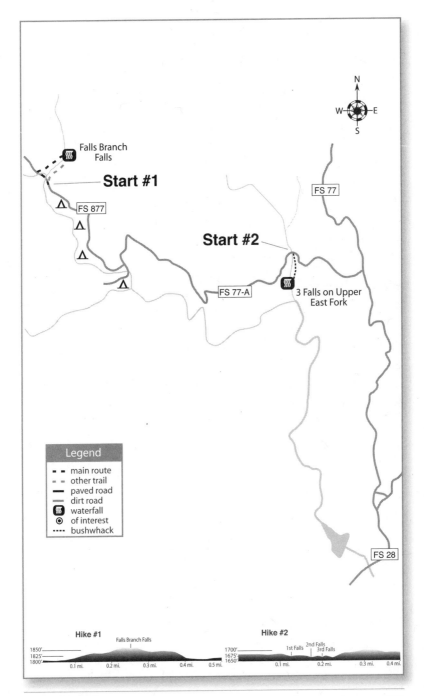

Falls Branch
Falls

Start #1

△ FS 877
△
△
△

FS 77

Start #2

FS 77-A

3 Falls on Upper
East Fork

N
W—E
S

Legend
- - main route
- - other trail
— paved road
— dirt road
🌊 waterfall
◉ of interest
···· bushwhack

FS 28

Hike #1
Falls Branch Falls
1850'
1825'
1800'
0.1 mi. 0.2 mi. 0.3 mi. 0.4 mi. 0.5 mi.

Hike #2
1st Falls 2nd Falls
3rd Falls
1700'
1675'
1650'
0.1 mi. 0.2 mi. 0.3 mi. 0.4 mi.

Bearden Falls Trail

Hike Distance:	3.1 mile
Type of Hike:	Out & Back
Number of Falls:	3
Hiking Time:	Half day
Dry Feet:	No
Start Elevation:	2,000 ft
Total Ascent:	513 ft
Land Manager:	USFS
Fee:	None

BEARDEN FALLS
Class: Tiered Height: 200 ft Rating: Spectacular

*B*ig payoff. That's what you get for your efforts on this hike. Bearden Falls is 200 feet, if not higher. Tucked away around the corner just behind Amicalola Falls State Park, this jewel of the Chattahoochee National Forest is relatively easy to get to by car, and the walk to the falls is nice, too. Think of it as one of three sisters—first there is big sister Amicalola at 729 feet, the tallest in Georgia. Next is middle sister Cochrans, easily 600 feet or higher. Finally there's little sister Bearden, 200 feet high at the least. Look on a topo map and you'll see all three in close proximity to each other, all falling off the same high escarpment bridging Frosty and Black Mountains.

On the drive into Beardens you'll pass quite a few roadside campsites. The Forest Service refers to this as dispersed roadside camping, and it is one of the best-kept camping secrets in Georgia. All across the top of the state are gravel roads maintained by the Forest Service. Drive up and down enough of them, and you'll quickly figure out that finding a place to plop a tent down for the night is pretty easy, and it's also free. Do you get a picnic table, flush toilets, garbage cans, and a shower? No. But you do get relative solitude and a scenic flat spot to set up your tent near the road. Most likely there's a stream nearby. Rarely are the campsites marked on any map; you just seem to happen upon one while driving down the road. If you're the kind of person who likes to throw caution to the wind, next time you head up into the hills, skip the lodge, the rental cabin, or the manicured campground with pulsing generators, and give one of these a try. You just have to head out and see what you can find.

The hike to view Bearden Falls is a snap, but you'll have to get your feet wet a few times while fording the creek. At just over three miles in all, it's long enough to air out your lungs and stretch your legs, but not long enough to wear you out. In fact, you might want to make this excursion part of the Three Sisters Roundup (p. 282). Start here and work your way up to big sister Amicalola or do it the other way around, whichever best fits your day.

WATERSLIDE ON BEARDEN CREEK
Class: Waterslide Height: 12 ft Rating: Fair

Bearden Falls Trail (cont.)

Getting to the Trailhead

From Nimblewill Baptist Church on Nimblewill Church Road east of Dahlonega via GA 52, drive east on Nimblewill Gap Road which becomes FS 28-2. At 2.3 miles the road turns to dirt. From here, continue another 2.2 miles to where the unmarked FS 28-E exits to the right. This is just before FS 28-2 begins to climb the mountain. Turn down this road and park at the large camping site on the right to start the hike.

GPS Coordinates

N 34° 35.35' W 84° 11.54'

Hiking Directions

Begin Walk out from the campsite and continue on FS 28-E. You will immediately cross a small stream.

Mile 0.4 The road ends here. Ford Nimblewill Creek and bear left upstream on a worn ATV track. A sign here reads, "no ATVs," but it's clear they use it anyhow.

Mile 0.6 Ford Bearden Creek just above where it enters Nimblewill Creek. Turn right at the trail fork and walk up alongside Bearden Creek. You'll soon enter a small, dark hemlock grove.

Mile 0.8 Look for a long, 12-foot-high waterslide off the left side of the trail.

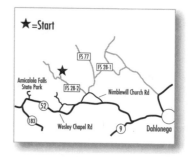

Mile 1.2 Here a small feeder stream makes a 20-foot-high, broken-tier cascade into Bearden Creek. With good flow this is a very attractive falls.

Mile 1.5 The trail becomes a footpath here and gets pretty steep. You are now approaching the absolute base of the falls.

Mile 1.55 Enjoy the view; Bearden Falls is crashing right down to you here. Return the way you came.

Mile 3.1 Finish.

FEEDER STREAM WATERFALL
Class: Tiered   Height: 20 ft   Rating: Nice

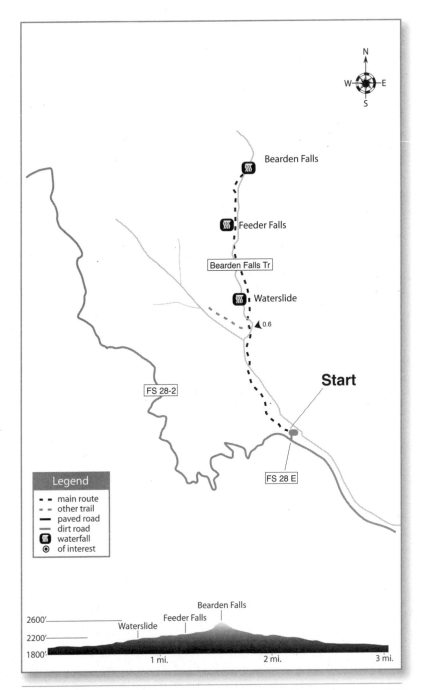

Bearden Falls

Feeder Falls

Bearden Falls Tr

Waterslide

▲0.6

Start

FS 28-2

FS 28 E

Legend
- - main route
- - other trail
— paved road
— dirt road
▨ waterfall
◉ of interest

2600'
Waterslide   Feeder Falls   Bearden Falls
2200'
1800'
1 mi.   2 mi.   3 mi.

Cochrans Falls

Hike Distance:	5.0 miles
Type of Hike:	Out & Back
Number of Falls:	1 giant
Hiking Time:	Half day
Dry Feet:	No
Start Elevation:	1,674 ft
Total Ascent:	700 ft
Land Manager:	USFS
Fee:	None

COCHRANS FALLS (A MIDDLE SECTION)
Class: Tiered Height: 600 ft Rating: Spectacular

You might decide to call this Frustrating Falls. It's spectacular, it's amazing, it's nearly as high as Amicalola Falls. It's the second-highest falls in Georgia and fifth-highest in the East. But without a helicopter, it's next to impossible to see all of Cochrans Falls. Waterfalls like Cochrans drop hundreds of feet through dense hanging forest and—with the exception of Amicalola Falls, which has a staircase next to it so you can see the whole thing—can be seen only in sections. The great thing about Cochrans Falls is that just one of its small sections alone would be considered a really high waterfall anywhere else.

The scenery on the way to the base of Cochrans Falls is a study in contrasts. The route follows the creek all the way, and it's a beautiful stream—clear, cold, and full of smooth, moss-covered rocks. No doubt there are plenty of trout hiding in the shaded green pools. All around are hardwoods and hemlock and the ever-present rhododendron. Looking about, it's all very pretty. At the other end of the spectrum, the roadbed you're walking on is anything but beautiful. It has become a destination for off-road vehicles (ORVs). These are the jacked-up pick-up trucks you've seen rumbling down the road. This road also sees many ATVs. These are the smaller 3- and 4-wheelers that you ride like a motorcycle. Together, they've made a complete mess of the old road. Along the way you'll see where they've ripped their way through the woods, creating a tangle of paths that all seem to converge back into one. There are huge mud pits, some filled with stagnant water and deep enough to swallow a truck. Small trees are bent over and others have had their bark stripped off where vehicles have forced their way through the narrow openings

COCHRANS FALLS (ANOTHER MIDDLE SECTION)
Much of the falls is hidden in the trees

between them. Unfortunately, you just have to put up with this scene to get to Cochrans Falls. As far as the actual walking goes, it's pretty easy going.

Once you pass the last campsite and near the falls, all the mess is quickly forgotten. You'll walk on an unmarked but well-trodden footpath with no sign of motor vehicle use. The falls itself cascades through a deep, V-shaped cleft in the mountain, the forested sides of which are nearly vertical. Don't even think about trying to make it all the way to the top. Enjoy the sections you can see, and then head back the way you came.

LOWER TIER OF COCHRANS FALLS
It just keeps going up from here

Cochrans Falls (cont.)

Getting to the Trailhead

On GA 52, 4.0 miles east of Amicalola Falls State Park or 14.5 miles west of Dahlonega, turn onto the westernmost end of Wesley Chapel Road. Drive 1.0 mile and turn left on Dan Fowler Road. Go 1.2 miles, turn left on Blackhawk Road and immediately ford a creek. Continue another 0.3 mile and park on the right just before the next creek ford. **Caution:** Creek ford on Blackhawk Road.

GPS Coordinates

N 34° 33.47' W 84° 12.14'

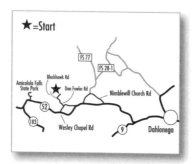

Hiking Directions

Begin Continuing on foot on the same road you drove in on, you'll immediately ford the creek and then ford it again at the next fork in the road. It is possible to drive this section, but after the second ford there is nowhere to park a car, so it is best to walk.

Mile 0.4 A road enters from the left. Continue to the right on the tangle of ORV tracks.

Mile 1.2 A road forks off to the left here and fords Cochrans Creek. Stay to the right.

Mile 1.8 You'll reach a camping spot in a pretty hemlock grove. The trail continues out the far side and is less worn here, but still shows ATV use.

Mile 1.9 Reach another camping spot. The ATV use ends here but a foot trail continues to climb up beside the creek.

Mile 2.2 Here you'll find the bottom drops of Cochrans Falls. They appear as a two-tiered, 30-foot falls through boulders and rhodo. You should be able to safely continue another couple of hundred yards up from here.

Mile 2.3+ More tiers of Cochrans Falls: a 30-foot slide followed by a 30-foot tiered sluice. You can see where folks have continued on up the rugged slope in an attempt to see the whole thing. Don't try it. It's very steep and it's treacherous. People have died here trying to see just a little more of the falls. Turn around and head back the way you came.

Mile 5.0 Finish.

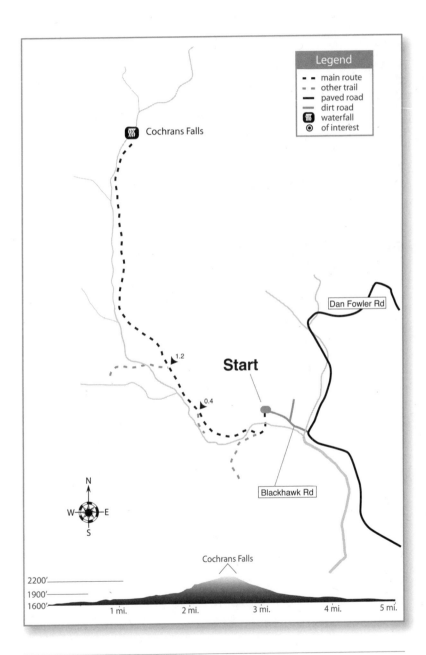

Cochrans Falls

Legend
- main route
- other trail
— paved road
— dirt road
🌊 waterfall
⊙ of interest

1.2

Start

0.4

Dan Fowler Rd

Blackhawk Rd

N
W E
S

Cochrans Falls

2200'
1900'
1600'
1 mi.   2 mi.   3 mi.   4 mi.   5 mi.

Amicalola Falls Loop

Hike Distance:	2.5 miles
Type of Hike:	Loop
Number of Falls:	1 giant
Hiking Time:	2 hours
Dry Feet:	Yes
Start Elevation:	1,841 ft
Total Ascent:	803 ft
Land Manager:	State Park
Fee:	$3

AMICALOLA FALLS
Class: Tiered Height: 729 ft Rating: Spectacular

This is it, the big one. This is Georgia's highest waterfall and probably its most famous. At 729 feet, it's not only the highest falls in Georgia, it's the third-highest in the eastern United States. No wonder an entire state park bears its name.

Given the popularity of Amicalola Falls, you can't expect solitude here on any visit. You can drive right up to the reflecting pool at the falls' base, and you can drive right to its very top. An observation platform up there looks out over the very lip of the waterfall, and it's quite a view. In between, a huge staircase leads you beside, over—everything but under—all the way along the course of the falls. Many of the people you're likely to meet on the "trail" are not what you would call hikers. Expect to see folks in footwear ranging from flip-flops to high heels. And don't be surprised if you see teenagers walking along with their heads down, texting on their cell phones while this amazing waterfall cascades down just over their shoulders. Signs tell just how many stairsteps to expect and warn against overexertion. It's certainly a contrast to just about any waterfall deep in the Cohutta Wilderness.

The trail heading up the steps and along the course of the falls is also the very beginning of the approach trail to the long-distance Appalachian Trail. In March, April, and May, several thousand hikers shoulder their gear and walk up these very steps to begin their journey to Maine. The official southern terminus is atop Springer Mountain, an 8.5-mile hike from the state park, and to get there, you must begin right here. If you're visiting at that time of year, chances are you'll see quite a few of these "thru-hikers," as they are known. They should be easy to spot with their heavy boots and full packs.

Inside the visitor center at the bottom of the mountain is a small museum that tells all about the AT and those who have hiked it and answers many of the questions you might have about its origin. You can also purchase maps, guidebooks, and any other small items you need.

On this particular route, you'll hike up the steps alongside the falls, cross over at the top, and come back down the mountain on the appropriately named East Ridge Trail. The views from the top and along East Ridge Trail are stunning, and chances are you'll see fewer people on the way back down.

TOP OF AMICALOLA FALLS
The observation deck provides a top-down view of the waterfall

Amicalola Falls Loop (cont.)

Getting to the Trailhead

Park and start at the trailhead parking lot in front of the information center, just beyond the entrance, in Amicalola Falls State Park. The park is between Ellijay and Dahlonega on GA 52.

GPS Coordinates

N 34° 33.50′ W 84° 14.97′

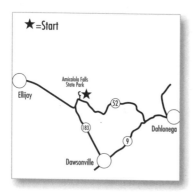

Hiking Directions

Begin Hike up the blue-blazed Appalachian Trail approach trail, which begins directly behind the visitor center.

Mile 0.6 Pass the reflecting pool. Facing the falls with the pool in between, you should be able to see an inverted image of the waterfall.

Mile 0.75 Here begins a section of 175 steps, taking you up and over the bottom tiers of the waterfall.

Mile 0.95 The first set of steps ends here at a bridge over the falls. It offers a great view of the

top section. Just ahead you'll turn to the right and continue up the last 425 steps.

Mile 1.2 Top of the falls. Bear right across the platform overlooking the lip of the falls and walk up to the upper parking lot toilets, where you'll turn right and head off the side of the mountain on East Ridge Trail. At this point it is an old roadbed.

Mile 1.8 Bear right off the roadbed onto a foot trail.

Mile 2.4 Close the loop where the trails meet behind the visitor center.

Mile 2.5 Finish back at the hiker parking lot.

AMICALOLA FALLS
600 steps ascend to the top of the falls

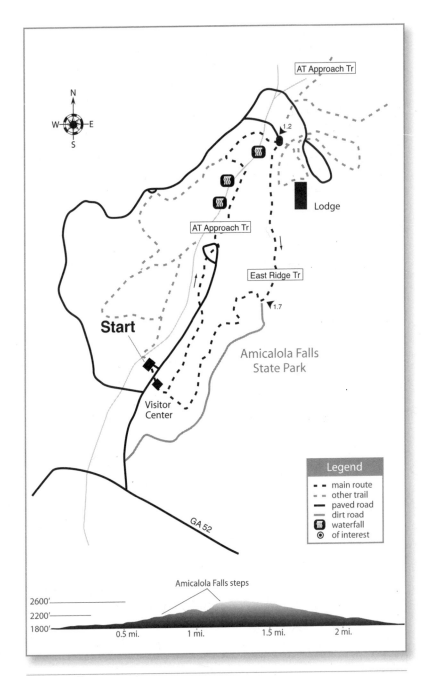

AT Approach Tr

1.2

Lodge

AT Approach Tr

East Ridge Tr

1.7

Start

Amicalola Falls
State Park

Visitor
Center

Legend

- - main route
- - other trail
— paved road
— dirt road
waterfall
of interest

N
W E
S

GA 52

Amicalola Falls steps

2600'
2200'
1800'

0.5 mi.   1 mi.   1.5 mi.   2 mi.

Edge of the World Loop

Hike Distance:	2.9 miles
Type of Hike:	Loop
Number of Falls:	1
Hiking Time:	2 hours
Dry Feet:	Yes
Start Elevation:	1,261 ft
Total Ascent:	565 ft
Land Manager:	GA DNR
Fee:	None

EDGE OF THE WORLD RAPID
Class: Rapid Height: 15 ft Rating: Good

Did you ever guess you could hike right out to the edge of the world? Who'd have thought that elusive place was right here in north Georgia? It may seem like an odd name for a rapid, but when you climb into a canoe and paddled down from the bridge, the perspective is a little different. All of a sudden the river abruptly disappears, and there's nothing but a horizon line and roaring whitewater. It looks like the edge of the world—and *that* is where the name came from.

In 1972 the movie *Deliverance*, based on a novel by James Dickey and starring Jon Voight, Burt Reynolds, Ronny Cox, and Ned Beatty, debuted across America. Rarely has a single movie had such an impact. Almost single-handedly it launched the whitewater industry in the South as we know it today, including whitewater rafting, kayaking, and canoe-ing. In the movie, four men from Atlanta blindly paddle down a remote river in the mountains of north Georgia, where they run into all sorts of trouble. The fictitious river's name is the Cahulawassee which, as the story goes, is soon to be dammed to create a lake. The four men figure this is a chance to see it before everything is covered with water. Most of the filming was done on the Chattooga and Tallulah Rivers on Georgia's northeastern border, but the real-life river that inspired the plot was the Coosawattee River, which, like the fictitious one, is now mostly buried under a lake—Carters Lake near Ellijay.

Soon after the movie was released, people began to flock to the rivers of north Georgia, paddling pretty much anything that would float. More than a few of them drowned in difficult rapids like Edge of the World. However, people are persistent, and it didn't take folks too long to figure out what types of craft worked best and what kinds of skills they needed to successfully negotiate the drops. Today, whitewater boats are made from space-age plastics, and paddling skill levels are such that experts can negotiate roaring waterfalls upwards of 40 feet high.

On this hike you'll follow a route originally mapped out as part of an Eagle Scout service project. Informative signs along the way point out various aspects of the woodlands, taking the learning notch up a level. The trail is well marked and fairly easy, save for a steep hill right at the beginning. You'll walk through a mixed pine and hardwood forest with seasonal huckleberries and blackberries interspersed through the understory. And by the time you reach Edge of the World rapid, you'll have earned a rest on the rocks by the big drop.

EDGE OF THE WORLD RAPID
Class: Rapid Height: 15 ft Rating: Good

Edge of the World Loop (cont.)

Getting to the Trailhead

From Dawsonville, drive 6.5 miles on GA 53 to the trailhead parking area, located on the right just before Amicalola Creek crosses under the highway.

GPS Coordinates

N 34° 25.59' W 84° 12.72'

Hiking Directions

Begin Walk down the steps from the parking lot and turn left on the boardwalk trail beside the river, heading downstream.

Mile 0.1 Pass under the highway bridge, turn left, and follow the blue-blazed trail up the hill.

Mile 0.3 A trail enters from the left. Continue straight on.

Mile 0.9 Turn right on the gravel forest road.

Mile 1.0 Turn right off the forest road, following blue blazes.

Mile 1.2 You'll find a picnic table here as well as a marble memorial to Jason Funk, a Boy Scout, now deceased, who worked on this trail for his Eagle Scout project.

Mile 1.9 Pass a spring.

Mile 2.5 Drop down onto the boardwalk trail. The Edge of the World is right in front of you—the rapid, that is. After viewing the rapid, continue on up the board-walk trail back to the parking lot.

Mile 2.9 Finish.

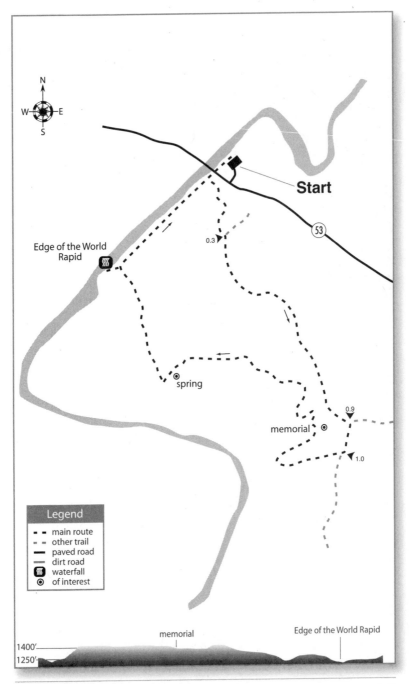

Wildcat Tract Loop

Hike Distance:	12.1 miles
Type of Hike:	Loop
Number of Falls:	6+
Hiking Time:	Full day
Dry Feet:	No
Start Elevation:	1,486 ft
Total Ascent:	2,835 ft
Land Manager:	GA DNR
Fee:	None

SECOND FALLS ON ROCKY FORD CREEK (BOTTOM)
Class: Sluice Height: 70 ft Rating: Excellent

This is one of the more difficult hikes in this book and certainly the longest. It includes a major three-mile climb, with a couple of really steep pitches, that just seems to go on forever. The reward? Six major waterfalls, with a few small ones thrown in for good measure.

The Wildcat Tract is part of the greater Dawson Forest Wildlife Management Area. If you've done the Edge of the World Loop (p. 138), you've hiked in the Amicalola Tract. Dawson Forest has four tracts, and they all follow the course of Amicalola Creek down to the Etowah River, south of Dawsonville. Thanks to the volunteer group Mountain Stewards, you'll find a network of superbly maintained hiking trails here with signs at all trail intersections and easy-to-see blazes on the trees.

Waterfall hikers to this area can choose which falls they want to visit based on their fitness level and the amount of time available. This route takes in all the falls on the tract within sight of a trail, and it requires a high level of hiking fitness—as well as most of a day. The difficulty is due to its total distance and the long, steep uphill. Twelve miles is a long day hike in anyone's book. Realize, also, that you will need to ford Wildcat Creek on the upper end. It's a good-sized stream, but there are typically ropes strung across to hold onto if you need them. If you're interested in an easier hike to just three of the falls, see p. 146.

You'll start out alongside tranquil Wildcat Creek and soon turn up the mountain alongside Rocky Ford Creek to view its waterfalls. The two highest are right on top of each other, a cascade mix of tiers and sluices that requires viewing from several vantage points to see the whole thing.

The trail then takes you up and over the mountain to the next

SECOND FALLS ON ROCKY FORD CREEK (TOP)
Class: Tiered Height: 70 ft Rating: Excellent

watershed of Fall Creek—a good name, because "fall" is exactly what it does. Over the course of three miles you'll see four astounding waterfalls. The first is just off the trail, the second and fourth are on short spur trails, and the third requires a short bushwhack back upstream to get to its base. You'll return along the length of Wildcat Creek.

Pictures of the other three falls on this hike are shown on pp. 146-148.

FIRST FALLS ON FALL CREEK
Class: Tiered Height: 20 ft Rating: Good

Wildcat Tract Loop (cont.)

Getting to the Trailhead

From Amicalola Falls State Park, travel west on GA 52 for 1.5 miles and bear left on GA 183. Drive 1.2 miles and turn right on GA 136. Continue 1.6 miles and turn left on Steve Tate Highway. Go 2.2 miles and turn right on Wildcat Campground Road. Drive 1.0 mile all the way to the back of the campground to the trailhead.

GPS Coordinates

N 34° 29.74' W 84° 16.93'

Hiking Directions

Begin Walk out of the back of the campground on Wildcat Creek Trail beside the creek.

Mile 1.7 Turn left across the footbridge onto Turner Trail.

Mile 2.0 Turn right on Rocky Ford Trail to begin climb.

Mile 2.4 Just before Windy Ridge Trail exits left, a goatpath on the right leads down to the first and second falls on Rocky Ford Creek. You'll hear them before

you see them. The first is a 12-foot waterslide. Fifty feet farther downstream is a much higher tiered sluice falling 70 feet. After viewing, continue on up Rocky Ford Trail.

Mile 4.2 You've made a very steep climb to here. Turn left on Tobacco Pouch Trail. You're not to the top quite yet.

Mile 4.6 Gate. Continue straight on.

Mile 5.3 Turn right, downhill (yes!) on Fall Creek Trail an old roadbed.

Mile 5.6 Just before the roadbed crosses the creek, turn right on a foot trail.

Mile 6.2 Ford Fall Creek. The first falls, a 20-footer, is on the right immediately after the ford.

Mile 6.9 The trail heads away from the creek for a while and climbs to this point. Turn right down an old gravel roadbed.

Mile 7.2 Bear left at the fork, go down the hill to the creek, and at the sign turn right on a short spur trail up to the second falls on Fall Creek. This is the highest of the four—a tiered drop of 80 feet. From here, continue down the creek.

Mile 8.0 Just below the creek ford here is the top of the third falls. It's best to see it from the bottom (and it's close to impossible to see from here), so continue on down the trail.

Mile 8.3 You are in a cove. To get back to the bottom of the third falls, you'll have to bushwhack back upstream alongside the creek. The going is not difficult; work your way around the rhodo thickets, and in about 100 yards you'll find yourself at the bottom of a 50-foot waterfall. From here continue back to the trail and on downstream.

Mile 9.0 Tobacco Pouch Trail enters from the right. Bear left.

Mile 9.4 Just before reaching Wildcat Creek Trail, turn back left on a spur trail to the fourth falls.

Mile 9.6 Fourth falls on Fall Creek, a 60-foot drop. Return to Wildcat Creek Trail and head downstream.

Mile 10.0 Ford Wildcat Creek. There are ropes here to help you.

Mile 10.4 Pass the footbridge you crossed earlier. Stay left.

Mile 12.1 Finish.

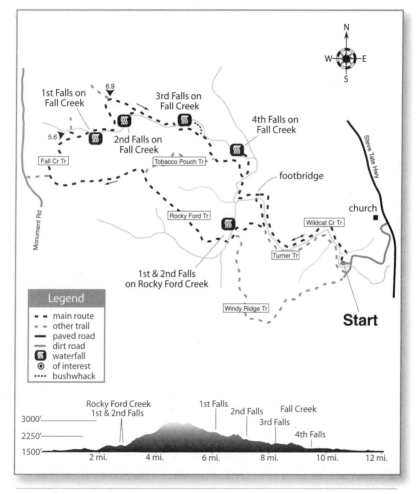

Wildcat Creek Trail

Hike Distance:	8 miles
Type of Hike:	Out & Back
Number of Falls:	3
Hiking Time:	Half day +
Dry Feet:	No
Start Elevation:	1,486 ft
Total Ascent:	600 ft
Land Manager:	GA DNR
Fee:	None

FOURTH FALLS ON FALL CREEK
Class: Tiered Height: 60 ft Rating: Excellent

Are you looking for another way to see some of the magnificent waterfalls in Dawson Forests Wildcat Tract? This is it. It's four miles shorter and a heck of a lot easier. You'll see half as many waterfalls, but three is good for any hike, and these three are pretty impressive.

Quite a few of the hikes in this book are on wildlife management areas, and most of these areas are also part of the Chattahoochee National Forest, where the land is managed for multiple uses. Dawson Forest, like Crockford–Pigeon Wildlife Management Area in the northwest part of the state, is a standalone area overseen by the Georgia Department of Natural Resources (DNR). People come here primarily to hunt and fish, and the land is managed specifically for those purposes.

You'll notice while you're hiking along that Wildcat Creek has a mix of gurgling shoals and quiet pools. This is ideal trout water. Fish line up where the fast water rushes into the slow water like students in a cafeteria line, taking their pick of tasty morsels as insect nymphs and larvae drift cluelessly within striking distance. Crafty fishermen take advantage of this and cast their hand-tied flies in those spots, hoping they will resemble the real thing enough to entice the trout to bite. It's fun to watch anglers stealthily casting their lines into the stream.

On specific days each fall the Wildlife Commission opens the Dawson Forest Tracts to hunters. If you're thinking of taking a hike here during that time of year, you'll definitely want to check out the hunting schedule in the Georgia Hunting Seasons and Regulations pamphlet. These are available for free at most sporting goods stores, or you can get the same information at www.gohuntgeorgia.com. On designated days, especially during deer season, the woods are likely to be full of hunters, and you will want to be elsewhere.

The three waterfalls you'll see on this hike are all on Fall Creek. The first one you get to is the fourth drop on the stream, as you'll encounter them from the bottom up. It drops 60 feet over three distinct tiers. Next is the third falls, and unlike the other two, you'll have to bushwhack along the stream from below the drop in order to see it. Since there is really nothing to tell you when you should head off the trail while walking from this direction, you may well walk past it on the way to the second falls on Fall Creek. You'll hear the third falls down the hill, which will help you find it on your way back. It's a pretty 50-foot slide.

The second falls on Fall Creek—the last one you'll come to and the highest of the lot—is a tiered drop falling 80 feet into a big pool. It's a great final destination and a good place to turn around, as the trail only gets steeper from here.

SECOND FALLS ON FALL CREEK
Class: Tiered Height: 80 ft Rating: Excellent

Getting to the Trailhead

From Amicalola Falls State Park, travel west on GA 52 for 1.5 miles and bear left on GA 183. Drive 1.2 miles and turn right on GA 136. Continue 1.6 miles and turn left on Steve Tate Highway. Go 2.2 miles and turn right on Wildcat Campground Road. Drive 1.0 mile all the way to the back of the campground to the trailhead.

GPS Coordinates
N 34° 29.74' W 84° 16.93'

THIRD FALLS ON FALL CREEK
Class: Slide Height: 50 ft Rating: Excellent

You'll pass a beaver pond on the way there.

Mile 2.4 The spur trail brings you to the fourth falls on Fall Creek, a 60-footer. Return to Fall Creek Trail and turn right.

Mile 3.1 You'll probably walk right past the place where you'll need to bushwhack up to see the third falls and realize it only when you hear the falls crashing loudly below the right side of the trail. Make a mental note of where you are and visit it on your return. See mileposts 8.0 and 8.3 on p. 144 for specific directions to the third falls.

Mile 4.0 A spur trail with a sign turns off to the left to take you to the base of the second falls on Fall Creek. This is the highest of the bunch at 80 feet, with a pool at the bottom. Return to the

Hiking Directions

Begin Walk out of the back of the campground on Wildcat Creek Trail beside the creek.

Mile 1.7 You'll pass a footbridge here. Stay to the right on Wildcat Creek Trail.

Mile 2.1 Ford Wildcat Creek. There are ropes here to help you. Just a little ways after crossing the creek, the trail forks. Take the right fork. This is the spur trail to the fourth falls on Fall Creek.

trailhead the way you came. If
you missed the third falls on the
hike in, be sure to check it out on
the return.

Mile 8.0 Finish.

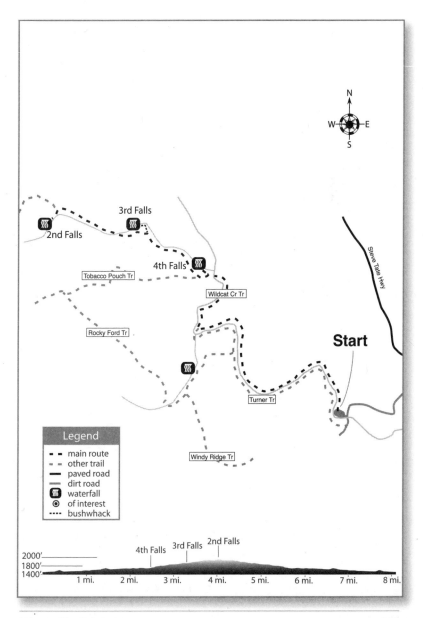

Eastern Blue Ridge

SECOND FALLS ON DODD CREEK EN ROUTE TO RAVEN CLIFFS

Eastern Blue Ridge Road Map with Falls

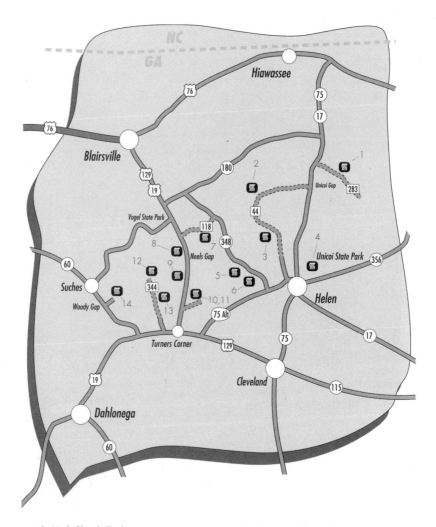

1. High Shoals Trail
2. Horsetrough Falls
3. Low Gap Creek Falls
4. Anna Ruby Falls Trail
5. Raven Cliffs Trail
6. Dukes Creek Falls Trail
7. Helton Creek Falls Trail
8. Blood Mountain Loop
9. Desoto Falls Trail
10. Little Ridge Creek Falls
11. Cowrock Creek Falls
12. Blood Mountain Creek Falls
13. Crow Mountain Creek Falls
14. Dockery Lake Trail

The region that makes up Georgia's eastern Blue Ridge is demarcated roughly from the towns of Dahlonega and Helen north to Blairsville and Hiawassee. In these hills are four wilderness areas—Mark Trail, Brasstown, Raven Cliffs, and Blood Mountain. Traversing the area on its northward track is the Appalachian Trail. Here, too, is Georgia's highest peak. At 4,668 feet, it stands apart from the main dividing ridge. Its summit provides a commanding view.

Outdoor lovers have flocked to the region for generations, drawn by the cool summer temperatures and abundant natural wonders. These days, many visitors are drawn to the artificial attractions found in Helen and Dahlonega.

Waterfall lovers have possibly the best reason to come here. It's hard to beat hikes like the one to Raven Cliffs Falls or Dockery Lake Trail where you can see five or six outstanding waterfalls all in one afternoon. Some of the falls in the area are so spectacular, they are tourist destinations in their own right. Take a stroll up to Anna Ruby Falls or down to

Dukes Creek Falls and you're likely to meet quite a few others along the way. On the other hand, if you walk up to the high waterfall on Crow Mountain Creek or venture off the beaten track to see if you can find the uppermost waterfall on Blood Mountain Creek, your chances of seeing someone else are rare.

Some of these hikes are in close proximity to one or two others, and don't take too long to complete. If you want to knock off more than one in a day, be sure to check out the suggested itineraries on p. 282.

BELOW THE GROTTO AT RAVEN CLIFFS FALLS

High Shoals Trail

Hike Distance:	2.8 miles
Type of Hike:	Out & Back
Number of Falls:	3
Hiking Time:	Half day
Dry Feet:	Yes
Start Elevation:	2,873 ft
Total Ascent:	950 ft
Land Manager:	USFS
Fee:	None

HIGH SHOALS FALLS
Class: Fan Height: 125 ft Rating: Excellent

The source of the Hiwassee River is on the northern flanks of Rocky Mountain. In fact, you'll have to ford the Hiwasee on the way to this hike. The river does not go very far before it is joined by High Shoals Creek, its first main tributary. You'd think a creek with a name like that would have a series of shoals high up in the hills, and in a way, that's true. These shoals happen to be more of the vertical variety and fall approximately 175 feet.

The Native American word *Unicoi* roughly translates to mean "white," "foggy," or "hazy." Unicoi Gap, just up the road, is thus aptly named. Drive through here en route to High Shoals early in the morning and you'll see why; the whole area is frequently covered in a white cloud at that time of day. It can be somewhat disorienting. Here's what causes the fog: overnight—especially during the warmer months—cool air settles into the surrounding valleys. This cool air reacts with the warm, humid air that was heated during the preceding day, and the moisture precipitates out as fog. Until just after sunrise, the fog will lie low in the valley. Higher up it will still be clear, but as the day begins to warm, the fog will rise slowly up the mountainsides. If you're up early and your timing is good, you can get a jump-start on the day and see something really special as well. Get up high on a road or a trail, somewhere that looks out over the mountain ridges. When the conditions are just right, you'll find yourself gazing over a sea of white clouds with only the island-like tops of the mountains visible. It's definitely worth that early alarm. That white sea is the fog lifting. As it continues to lift, you'll be bathed in mist—and what just a moment ago *looked* cool, now literally *is* cool. Be

sure to carry a light sweater in your day pack.

High Shoals Trail starts plenty high enough that you might start out from the trailhead in just such a fog. It won't last; in most cases you'll either walk out from under it or it will just burn off. Enjoy it while you can—it imparts a certain eeriness to the woods, muffling ambient sounds so that all you hear is your own movements.

Both Blue Hole and High Shoals make great destination hikes most any time of year. On freezing winter days, huge icicles form along the cliff at High Shoals Falls. If it's hot out, be sure to allow time for a dip in the plunge pool below Blue Hole Falls. It's 20 feet deep—so cold and clear it looks blue. You may look blue, too, after a good soak therein.

BLUE HOLE FALLS
Class: Horsetail   Height: 30 ft   Rating: Good

High Shoals Trail (cont.)

Getting to the Trailhead

From Unicoi Gap on GA 17/75 north of Helen, drive north for 2.0 miles and turn right on FS 283. Ford the stream and continue another 1.3 miles to the trailhead, which is marked. **Caution:** Creek ford on FS 283.

GPS Coordinates
N 34° 48.97' W 83° 43.62'

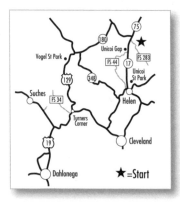

Top of Blue Hole Falls
Class: Tiered Height: 10 ft Rating: Fair

Mile 1.2 The trail splits here. Take the left fork, which is still marked with green blazes.

Mile 1.4 You should now have reached the viewing platform at the bottom of High Shoals Falls. What a waterfall! It drops 125 feet as it fans out over the rock cliff. Once you've had enough of it, return to the trailhead the way you came.

Mile 2.8 Finish.

Hiking Directions

Begin Walk downhill on the green-blazed trail.

Mile 0.7 Cross the creek on a wooden bridge.

Mile 1.0 Look down to your left and you can see the top drop of Blue Hole Falls. Directly below it is a 25-foot drop into a big blue plunge pool. Just beyond here a side trail leads to a viewing platform at the base of the falls. After a good look at this one, continue on down the trail.

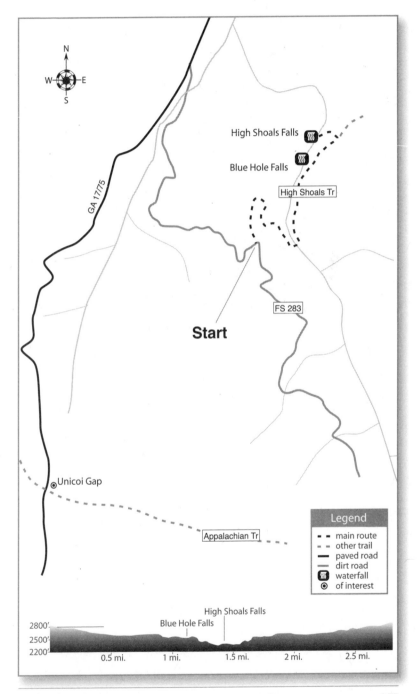

High Shoals Falls

Blue Hole Falls

High Shoals Tr

GA 17/75

FS 283

Start

Unicoi Gap

Appalachian Tr

Legend
- - - main route
- - - other trail
— paved road
— dirt road
🌊 waterfall
◉ of interest

High Shoals Falls

Blue Hole Falls

2800'
2500'
2200'

0.5 mi. 1 mi. 1.5 mi. 2 mi. 2.5 mi.

Horsetrough Falls

Hike Distance:	1 mile
Type of Hike:	Y-shape
Number of Falls:	2+
Hiking Time:	1 hour
Dry Feet:	Yes
Start Elevation:	2,357 ft
Total Ascent:	261 ft
Land Manager:	USFS
Fee:	None

HORSETROUGH FALLS
Class: Fan Height: 100 ft Rating: Excellent

High in the hills above the small faux-Bavarian village of Helen lie the headwaters of one of Georgia's mightiest and most important rivers—the Chattahoochee. Water that originates here goes on to fill six major reservoirs, providing drinking water for the city of Atlanta and electricity for millions in Georgia, Alabama, and Florida. In fact, the three states have waged costly court battles over who has the rights to its water. The Chattahoochee also serves as the state border between Alabama and Georgia before heading into Florida and Lake Seminole. From there it enters the Gulf of Mexico as the Apalachicola River. Looking at any one of the falls in the watershed, it's hard to imagine the sheer volume of water this river will take on as it moves toward the ocean.

Hydropower and drinking water weren't always the primary uses of the Chattahoochee. Nearly 200 years ago the river supported a thriving shipping industry, and steamboat trade made the city of Columbus, GA, a major cotton marketing center. Steamers could carry goods from the Gulf up the river as far north as the fall line just below Atlanta. Above that line a series of flatboats could haul the stuff into the city. King Cotton owed its power to a river that started high in the mountains.

This short hike packs in quite a lot and is ideal for most anyone who can move along on two feet. You'll walk just under a mile and see two really nice waterfalls. First up is Horsetrough Falls, a superb waterfall cascading 100

UPPER FALLS ON CHATTAHOOCHEE RIVER
Class: Slide Height: 25 ft Rating: Good

feet over the face of a cliff. You'll get a great view from a nicely built wooden platform. Not far away, on the small stream which, believe it or not, is the uppermost portion of the Chattahoochee, the river drops 25 feet through a slot no more than two feet wide. Here it is possible to cross the Chattahoochee River in a single hop. Don't try that in Atlanta!

Be sure to visit the three bonus falls near this route as well. They are the icing on the cake.

Bonus Falls

UPPER SPOILCANE CREEK FALLS
Class: Fan Height: 40 ft Rating: Fair

So close it almost lands in the road, this waterfall is located on the right side of FS 44, 0.3 mile from Unicoi Gap. You'll pass it en route to Horsetrough Falls.

Horsetrough Falls (cont.)

Bonus Falls

WILKS CREEK UPPER FALLS
Class: Tiered   Height: 40 ft
Rating: Good

Pay close attention to your mileage for these two. They are located 3.5 miles from Unicoi Gap on FS 44 as you head toward Horsetrough Falls. Look for them down off the left side of the road. It's a steep scramble down to the creek, so take care. One is located 30 yards downstream of the other.
GPS: N 34° 47.18' W 83° 46.19'.

WILKS CREEK LOWER FALLS
Class: Tiered   Height: 25 ft
Rating: Good

Getting to the Trailhead

From Unicoi Gap on GA 17/75 north of Helen, take FS 44 for 4.8 miles. Turn right into Upper Chattahoochee River Campground. The trailhead is at the far end at the day-use area.

GPS Coordinates
N 34° 47.49' W 83° 47.08'

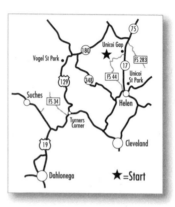

Hiking Directions

Begin From the trailhead, head onto the trail and almost immediately cross a footbridge, bearing left on the far side.

Mile 0.1 Viewing platform for Horsetrough Falls. After viewing the falls, go back to the bridge and turn left before crossing it onto a well-beaten path alongside the river. As you walk along you'll see slivers of whitewater through the woods to the right, below the trail.

Mile 0.5 Here is a 2-foot-wide cleft in the small cliff face where the entire upper Chattahoochee

River flushes through, then falls
25 feet. It's quite a sight. Return to
the trailhead from here.

Mile 1.0 Finish.

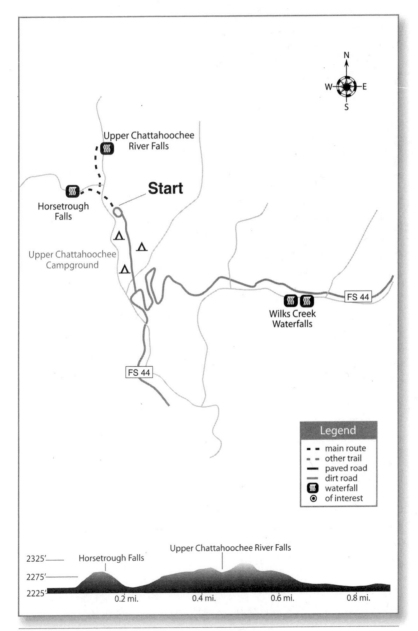

Low Gap Creek Falls

Hike Distance:	2 miles
Type of Hike:	Out & Back
Number of Falls:	3
Hiking Time:	2 hours
Dry Feet:	No
Start Elevation:	2,000 ft
Total Ascent:	538 ft
Land Manager:	USFS
Fee:	None

UPPER FALLS ON LOW GAP CREEK
Class: Slide/Plunge Height: 30 ft Rating: Good

You get a silver star if you make it all the way to the far end of this hike. The route (there is no designated trail) starts out with a stream ford and then heads upstream into a quick scramble above the creek. You can avoid this scramble by fording the creek to the old roadbed on the other side and then fording back again, but be forewarned—that side is filled with poison ivy. After this scramble, things even out for a short distance before you'll ford the creek for the last time at a confluence of streams. You'll then have to make your way on a goatpath, which you'll soon find out is better than no path at all—that's what's farther up the creek. This gets you to the first waterfall. There are two more to come, and they get better as you go up.

Soon after the first waterfall, it becomes a pick-your-own-route affair. The best alternative is to angle up a steep slope just before you reach a tangle of rhododendron and traverse the hillside above it. Traversing the hill is like walking across a steep-pitched roof, in that there's no real danger of a slip or fall; you mainly want to avoid getting hung up in all

LOWER FALLS ON LOW GAP CREEK
Class: Slide Height: 12 ft Rating: Fair

You have the option of a short bonus hike here as well. Just off FS 44 on the drive in, you'll pass over Double Culvert Branch. A short walk/scramble up the hill quickly brings you to two fairly high waterfalls. The first you'll see is a tiered 30-footer, and it's the easiest to get to. From its base, you can barely see the second, high up through the trees. Scramble up and around the first falls to get to the second, and you'll find a 40-foot plunge with an angled tier at the bottom. Not too bad for a 15-minute excursion.

that rhododendron down by the creek. One look at it and you can see why it is known among mountain folk as a "rhododendron hell." This is not a route where you need to fear getting lost. It's just a matter of to what extremes you're willing to go to see the waterfalls—thus the silver star award.

Be assured, the falls are well worth any difficulties you might encounter on your way to them. Sluices, pourovers, and vertical plunges are all mixed up together to make for some impressive drops; in the last, the creek slides beneath a huge overhanging boulder. Expect this hike to take a bit longer than your usual two-miler.

MIDDLE FALLS ON LOW GAP CREEK
Class: Fan Height: 15 ft Rating: Good

Low Gap Creek Falls (cont.)

Getting to the Trailhead

From Helen, drive 1.0 mile north on GA 17/75. Turn left onto Alt. 75. Cross the river and turn right onto FS 44. From here, at 2.9 miles you'll pass a game check station on the right. At 3.7 miles is the bonus Double Culvert Creek Falls on the left. At 4.2 miles go straight on FS 44A and through Low Gap Creek Campground another 0.8 mile to park before the second stream ford. **Caution:** Creek ford on FS 44A.

GPS Coordinates

N 34° 45.36′ W 83° 47.38′

★ =Start

Hiking Directions

Begin Ford the creek on foot and begin walking upstream, following a faint unmarked trail.

Mile 0.4 Two creeks merge here. Ford just downstream of the confluence and then make your way upstream on the right side of the right fork.

Bonus Falls

UPPER DOUBLE CULVERT BRANCH FALLS
Class: Tiered   Height: 40 ft
Rating: Good

These waterfalls are just off the left side of FS 44 at the 3.7 mile mark from its start near Helen. You'll see a rough trail heading up the left side of the Branch. The first is easiest to access, and you'll have to scramble a bit to see the upper falls. Round trip, you'll hike about half a mile to see them both.

GPS: N 34° 44.82′ W 83° 46.82′

LOWER DOUBLE CULVERT BRANCH FALLS
Class: Tiered   Height: 30 ft
Rating: Good

Mile 0.5 Reach Lower Low Gap Creek Falls, a 12-foot slide.

Mile 0.7 Pay attention now. You'll notice a small slide falls here, and the rhodo gets pretty thick. Angle uphill above the rhodo and just below a small tributary drip falls. Take care; this is barely a goatpath, and it's a steep slope to traverse.

Mile 0.9 Middle Low Gap Creek Falls, a 15-foot-high fan emptying into a small pool. You can see and hear it just before you get there. From the base, continue to work your way up the right shore.

Mile 1.0 Upper Low Gap Creek Falls, a 20-foot slide under a huge boulder culminating in a 10-foot plunge. Return the way you came.

Mile 2.0 Finish.

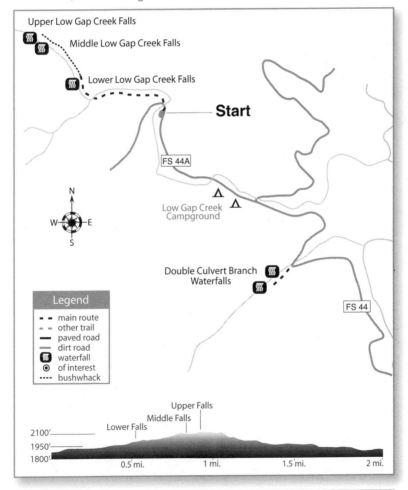

Anna Ruby Falls Trail

Hike Distance:	1 mile
Type of Hike:	Out & Back
Number of Falls:	2
Hiking Time:	1 hour
Dry Feet:	Yes
Start Elevation:	2,032 ft
Total Ascent:	250 ft
Land Manager:	USFS
Fee:	$2 pp

YORK CREEK FALLS AT ANNA RUBY
Class: Plunge Height: 50 ft Rating: Excellent

Let's be clear—this is not a wilderness hike. It's a popular short excursion to Anna Ruby Falls, a set of beautiful twin waterfalls—which happen to be two of the most famous in Georgia—located just outside Helen. Thousands of people flock here each year to walk up a paved trail to see the falls, and they pay $2 each for the experience. Along the way are interpretive signs describing the trees and wildflowers. These are somewhat overshadowed by conspicuous warning signs asking visitors to keep off the slippery rocks and out of the creek, and discouraging anyone from hiking the Smith Creek Trail lest they not make it back before the gate closes for the night. If you're looking for remote solitude, you won't find it here. But if you've got young children or don't feel up for climbing, this hike is for you.

Up until the late 1960s, Helen was a sleepy little north Georgia mountain town. Other than its idyllic location, there was nothing remarkable about it. That was before the transformation. Sometime about 1968, three businessmen came up with a plan to give Helen an extreme makeover. Their idea was to turn it into a Bavarian village and attract more tourists to the area. Drive through Helen today, and you can see that their idea was a grand success. People from all over the country flock there. A busy day (which can be any time of the year) sees wall-to-wall people on foot and in cars. Parking is at a premium, so cute trolleys ferry the nonwalkers from place to place as German polka music emanates from candy shops, leather shops, and wiener-schnitzel stands. You might say it's a little over the top, but people seem to be having a good time.

Most everyone in and around Helen has devised some plan for attracting tourist dollars. Of course there are the gazillion retailers in the heart of town where anything and everything seems to be for sale. If you're looking for a bite to eat, culinary options run the gamut. Need a place to stay the night? Not a problem. There's luxury lodging, camping, and everything in between. Need ideas for something to do? You can ride a go-cart, play mini-golf, take a ride in a hot air balloon, tube on the river, rent a bicycle, learn to cast a fly rod, cruise into the hills on your motorcycle, or just hang out and watch people all day long. You will not be bored.

Given all this, it makes perfect sense that today's Anna Ruby Falls is what it is. Long before the paved trail, the visitor center gift shop, and the entry fee, the falls itself was a popular destination for tourists visiting Helen. Paving the trail keeps it from getting worn down and eroded by so much foot traffic. Charging an entry fee helps finance the picnic tables, the garbage removal, and maintenance of the surrounding area. And the gift shop? Well, this *is* Helen, after all.

CURTIS CREEK FALLS AT ANNA RUBY
Class: Tiered Height: 153 ft Rating: Excellent

Getting to the Trailhead

From Helen, take GA 356 toward Unicoi State Park. Just before crossing the dam for Smith Lake and before the entrance to the beach access area, turn left on Anna Ruby Falls Road. It's 3.3 miles to the trailhead at the visitor center and gift shop. You'll pass through a pay station gate on the way in.

GPS Coordinates

N 34° 45.44' W 83° 42.60'

★ =Start

Hiking Directions

Begin The trail to the falls starts just to the left of the visitor center and gift shop. It's ridiculously easy to follow, paved the entire way, and has benches placed at intervals should you want to rest.

Mile 0.5 The trail ends at a large wooden viewing platform, built to hold quite a crowd. Here two waterfalls fall side by side. The one to your left is the highest at 153 feet, formed by Curtis Creek. The one on the right is 50 feet high and formed by York Creek. Together they are known as Anna Ruby Falls, but really they are two separate waterfalls. Their waters meet here to form Smith Creek. The 4.5-mile Smith Creek Trail, which begins on the far side of Unicoi State Park, terminates here. You'll see plenty of warning signs discouraging anyone from hiking this trail without some sort of transportation waiting on the other end. Makes you wonder why it was built in the first place. Return the way you hiked in.

Mile 1.0 Finish.

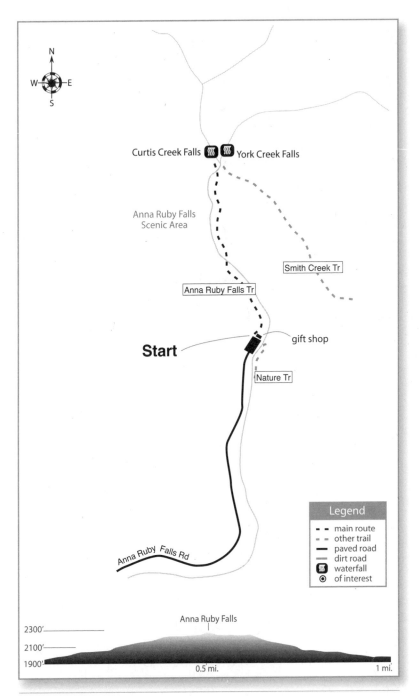

Curtis Creek Falls York Creek Falls

Anna Ruby Falls
Scenic Area

Smith Creek Tr

Anna Ruby Falls Tr

Start

gift shop

Nature Tr

Anna Ruby Falls Rd

Legend
- - main route
- - other trail
— paved road
— dirt road
🌊 waterfall
◉ of interest

Anna Ruby Falls

2300'
2100'
1900'
0.5 mi.   1 mi.

Raven Cliffs Trail

Hike Distance:	6 miles
Type of Hike:	Out & Back
Number of Falls:	6+
Hiking Time:	Half day +
Dry Feet:	Maybe
Start Elevation:	2,028 ft
Total Ascent:	1,200 ft
Land Manager:	USFS
Fee:	None

RAVEN CLIFFS FALLS   Class: Tiered Plunging Chute
Height: 170 ft Rating: Spectacular

On this hike you'll tramp to a fascinating waterfall. Raven Cliffs Falls is at the head of a waterfall-rich drainage area comprising Dodd Creek, Davis Creek, Bear Den Creek, and Little Low Gap Branch. These all flow down out of the Raven Cliffs and Mark Trail Wilderness Areas to form Dukes Creek. On Dodd Creek alone there are at least six waterfalls within a little over three miles. There are three more on Davis Creek, and Dukes Creek has a few as well. It's a great place to go for a day hike. With numerous campsites along the trail and elsewhere in the area, it can also make a nice overnight excursion.

Like many of the trails in the north Georgia mountains, much of Raven Cliffs Trail follows the route of an old railroad bed. These weren't ordinary train tracks for passenger trains. These were narrow gauge tracks built specifically for logging trains hauling timber out of the most remote sections of the state. Looking around at the lush vegetation and dense forest, it is hard to believe that these woods were once almost completely logged out.

SECOND FALLS ON DODD CREEK
Class: Plunge Height: 15 ft Rating: Good

Back around the turn of the 19th century, folks looked at the trees in these mountains with dollar signs in their eyes. Homesteaders who had once lived by cultivating the land realized they could make a much better living by first selling off most of their property to logging companies and then going to work as loggers themselves, clearing the forests of trees.

Early logging methods made for slow going. With a broadaxe, a logger did well to cut down and prepare one big tree per day. But with the invention of the two-person crosscut saw, it was possible to fell and process close to 50 trees a day. This one invention revolutionized the timber industry. By 1910 the South led the nation in lumber production, and the mills in the mountains of north Georgia were its biggest producers at 350 million board feet per year. The largest mill in the eastern United States was located in Helen, just down the road from Raven Cliffs Trail.

Early loggers took the largest and best trees in the forest. Only the sickly and damaged timber remained, leaving poor breeding

FIRST FALLS ON DODD CREEK
Class: Tiered Sluice Height: 15 ft Rating: Fair

Raven Cliffs Trail (cont.)

Bonus Falls

FALLS ON TRIBUTARY TO DAVIS CREEK
Class: Sluice   Height: 20 ft
Rating: Nice

You'll walk past this tributary falls above en route to the waterfall below it. Both are just off the right side of FS 344, 1.0 mile beyond the trailhead for Raven Cliffs Trail. Park just before the road fords Davis Creek and walk the short way up beside the creek to the waterfalls.

THIRD FALLS ON DAVIS CREEK
Class: Tiered   Height: 30 ft
Rating: Good

stock for future generations of trees. To get the logs to the mills, loggers sent the great felled tree trunks tearing down the steep mountainsides. Anything in the way was ripped from its roots, leaving the path open for erosion and disease. ·More trees meant more money, and before long there was little left on the slopes.

By this time, steam locomotion had progressed to a point where specially developed engines hauled heavily loaded flat cars of logs up and down steep grades. Sturdy narrow-gauge railways were constructed deep into the mountains to haul out the logs. The steam locomotives belched embers into the air, and the resulting wildfires were frequent and devastating. If not for the efforts of forest rangers in the 1920s and the Civilian Conservation Corps in the 1930s, the forests of north Georgia might never have recovered to their current beauty.

The hike up to Raven Cliffs Falls is a very popular excursion. Its proximity to Helen, ease of access, and natural beauty certainly contribute to its appeal. Unless you're out in the most inclement of weather, expect to see others walking on the trail or camping in one of the many backcountry campsites along the route. Before you've gone a mile you'll see the

THIRD FALLS ON DODD CREEK
Class: Horsetail Height: 30 ft Rating: Excellent

over a cliff. But you've still got some hiking to do yet.

Once you see it, there's no mistaking Raven Cliffs Falls. Dropping 170 feet over, under, and through a breach in the rock face, it's one of a kind. The most easily seen part is also the most dramatic. Far back in a six-foot-wide crack, the water makes a 40-foot freefall plunge into a dark green pool. This magical grotto is guarded above and below by rocks and water.

first of the falls, a 15-foot-high, tiered, riverwide drop into an angled sluice. Notice that the rocks are chock full of potholes, made by swirling pebbles and sand grinding away at the stone over the years. Potholes don't form overnight.

Farther up and about half-way to the cliffs is the second falls. Here the river plunges 15 feet, creating a horsetail, then slips another 15 feet down a long slide.

You don't have to hike too much farther to reach the third falls, and at this point many people think they've reached Raven Cliffs Falls. It's an easy mistake to make, since you're now in an area of cliffs, high above a 30-foot waterfall that careens

LOWER PORTION RAVEN CLIFFS FALLS
Class: Tiered Height: 170 ft Rating: Spectacular

Raven Cliffs Trail (cont.)

Getting to the Trailhead

From Helen, take GA 75 Alt. for 2.2 miles. Turn right on GA 348, drive 3.0 miles and turn left on FS 244 to the Raven Cliffs trailhead parking area.

GPS Coordinates
N 34° 42.57' W 83° 47.32'

★=Start

Hiking Directions

Begin Walk across FS 244 and onto Raven Cliffs Trail.

Mile 0.4 The first falls, a 15-footer, is on the left below the trail.

Mile 0.8 Pass a small, 8-foot broken sluice falls.

Mile 1.3 Second falls, a 15-foot plunge followed by a 15-foot slide.

Mile 1.6 You are now at a cliff area high above a 30-foot horsetail drop. You'll have to scramble to the base.

Mile 3.0 The trail reaches the absolute base of Raven Cliffs Falls

and then heads steeply up the hill beside it to a cleft in the cliff where the most dramatic part of the waterfall may be seen. The top is still a long way up, hidden between more rock clefts. You can see where people have scaled their way up trying to reach the top of the falls via a series of sketchy-looking, hand-over-hand, pull-yourself-up trails. Don't be tempted to try it. The view of the falls really does not

Bonus Falls

SECOND FALLS ON DAVIS CREEK
Class: Fan Height: 50 ft Rating: Good

This waterfall is located just 25 yards upstream of the lip of Dukes Creek Falls (p. 176). To see it, drive from the Raven Cliffs Falls trailhead parking area on FS 244 for 0.6 miles to a pullout on the left. Follow the short trail below the pullout down through a campsite to a flat spot just below this waterfall.

get any better than the one from the base of the cleft. Enjoy it, then head back the way you came.

Mile 6.0 Finish.

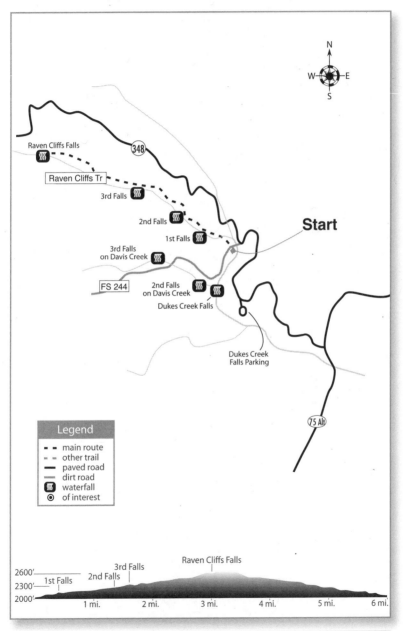

Dukes Creek Falls Trail

Hike Distance:	2.2 miles
Type of Hike:	Out & Back
Number of Falls:	2
Hiking Time:	2 hours
Dry Feet:	Yes
Start Elevation:	2,131 ft
Total Ascent:	400 ft
Land Manager:	USFS
Fee:	$3

DUKES CREEK FALLS ON DAVIS CREEK
Class: Tiered Height: 250 ft Rating: Excellent

If it's close to Helen, it's bound to be popular, and the hike to Dukes Creek Falls is just that. Next to Anna Ruby, the waterfalls at Dukes Creek are probably the most popular in the area. Even on the hottest summer days, the mist that fills the air all around the viewing platforms is cool and refreshing. Though you'll climb 400 feet in a mile on the way out, the hike itself is pretty easy. Trail builders made sure to keep the grade reasonable, so except for when you're climbing the series of steps near the top, you hardly know you're walking uphill. If you can walk around the block without tripping, you can do this hike.

Here's what to expect when you get to the trailhead. First, you'll pay a $3 parking fee. Like many of the fee areas in the national forest, you'll do this at a self-pay station. Basically, that means stuffing the cash (you need correct change; there are no ATMs here) in a colored envelope on which you write the date, your license plate information, and where you're from. There's a number on the envelope that corresponds to a number on a tear-off tag you'll hang on your vehicle's rearview mirror.

Once that necessary step is completed, you can look around for a parking space.

At the head of the parking lot is a nicely situated toilet building, well kept and clean. There are bear-proof trash cans in front of it, and just beyond is a fabulous view, with picnic tables off to one side. You get a lot for your $3 here.

The trail itself starts out paved, and it's just a short walk to a viewing platform, from which you get a long-distance view of Dukes Creek Falls. This is a much more open view than you'll have from the base of the falls. Davis Creek cascades over the lip of a high cliff and then spreads out like a spider web, sending channels of water in all directions to crash 250 feet into Dukes Creek below. Yes, you read it right. Dukes Creek Falls is actually on Davis Creek.

From the platform, you'll walk down a series of wooden steps to meet another trail coming in from the right (the people you see walking in from that direction are the ones who discovered that if you start at the Raven Cliffs trailhead instead, you save three dollars). From here, you'll hike first on a wide trail, then a narrow one. In a mile you'll be at the bottom of the falls where there are two large viewing platforms connected by a wooden walkway. You get a great view of a series of falls on Dukes Creek—and, of course, Dukes Creek Falls itself up through the trees. The number of people you're likely to see at the viewing platform is a testament to the popularity of this waterfall.

FALLS ON DUKES CREEK
Class: Tiered Height: 35 ft Rating: Good

Dukes Creek Falls Trail (cont.)

Getting to the Trailhead

From Helen, take GA 75 Alt. for 2.2 miles. Turn right on GA 348, drive 2.0 miles and turn left up the entrance road to the Dukes Creek Falls trailhead parking area.

GPS Coordinates

N 34° 42.11′ W 83° 47.34′

★ =Start

Hiking Directions

Begin Follow the paved trail which starts just to the right of the toilets.

Mile 0.1 An observation deck here offers a long-range view of Dukes Creek Falls for those who don't care to make the hike. Continue from here down a set of wooden steps.

Mile 0.3 Bottom of steps. A trail that begins near the Raven Cliffs trailhead parking area enters here. Make a hard turn back to the left to walk on a wide trail high above the creek. You can

hear and barely see several waterfalls crashing down below.

Mile 0.9 The trail narrows noticeably here as you continue your gradual descent.

Mile 1.1 Reach two wooden viewing platforms built to optimize the view of the falls. Dukes Creek Falls is right in front of you, crashing in all directions across a high cliff face. It's actually on Davis Creek. The other waterfall is on Dukes Creek proper and is also impressive. The bottoms of the two waterfalls meet, and the effect is stunning. Once you've had enough of the falling water, return the way you came.

Mile 2.2 Finish.

LOWER TIER OF DUKES CREEK FALLS

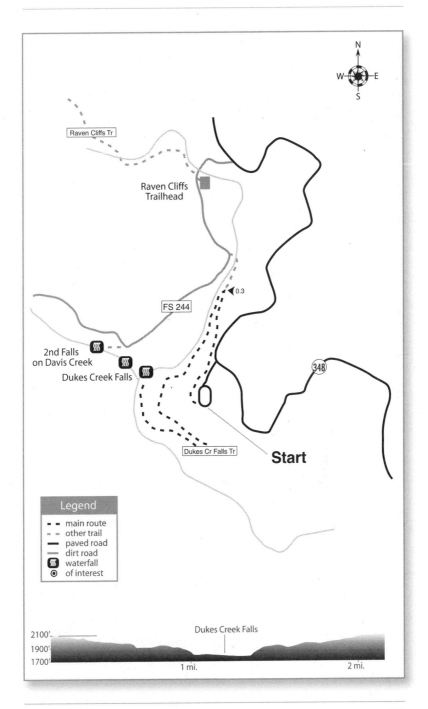

Raven Cliffs Tr

Raven Cliffs
Trailhead

FS 244

0.3

2nd Falls
on Davis Creek

Dukes Creek Falls

Dukes Cr Falls Tr

348

Start

N
W — E
S

Legend
- - main route
- - other trail
— paved road
— dirt road
waterfall
of interest

2100'
1900'
1700'

Dukes Creek Falls

1 mi.   2 mi.

Helton Creek Falls Trail

Hike Distance:	0.5 mile
Type of Hike:	Out & Back
Number of Falls:	2
Hiking Time:	1 hour
Dry Feet:	Yes
Start Elevation:	2,292 ft
Total Ascent:	150 ft
Land Manager:	USFS
Fee:	None

UPPER HELTON CREEK FALLS
Class: Tiered Height: 80 ft Rating: Excellent

More of a stroll than a hike, the walk down to this pair of falls on Helton Creek is still well worth the drive in on the bumpy forest road. You wouldn't want to drive all the way from Atlanta just for these, but if you're in the neighborhood, stop in for a visit and stretch your legs at the same time.

The first waterfall you'll see is a classic slide, dropping 40 feet. Part way down, a vertical rock sends the water spraying up in a roostertail. Just upstream is an even bigger waterfall, an 80-foot, two-tiered drop into a shallow pool.

LOWER HELTON CREEK FALLS
Class: Slide Height: 40 ft Rating: Good

Getting to the Trailhead

From Neels Gap north of Dahlonega on US 19/129, go north for 1.6 miles. Turn right on Helton Creek Road/FS 118. Drive 1.7 miles and go right at the road fork. It's 0.7 mile to the trailhead on the right.

GPS Coordinates

N 34° 45.19' W 83° 53.66'

Hiking Directions

Begin Take the trail toward the lower falls. It's just ahead of you.

Mile 0.1 Turn left off the trail to view the lower falls from its base.

Continue on up the trail to view the upper falls.

Mile 0.25 Step out onto the viewing platform for the upper falls. When you're ready, return the way you came.

Mile 0.5 Finish.

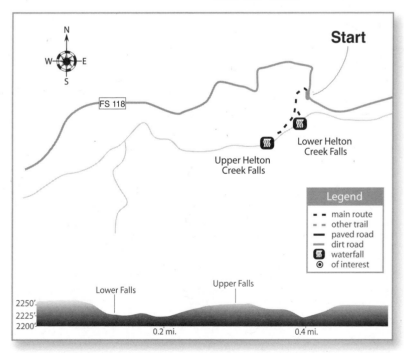

Blood Mountain Loop

Hike Distance:	7 miles
Type of Hike:	Loop
Number of Falls:	3
Hiking Time:	3/4 day
Dry Feet:	Maybe
Start Elevation:	3,013 ft
Total Ascent:	2,882 ft
Land Manager:	USFS
Fee:	None

UPPER FALLS ON BLOOD MOUNTAIN CREEK
Class: Segmented Height: 100 ft Rating: Excellent

Just how many waterfalls are there in the mountains of north Georgia? There are the famous ones—such as Amicalola, Anna Ruby, and Oceana. There are the ones on public lands with trails leading to them—Minnehaha, Jacks River, and Keown. There are even quite a few waterfalls on private land—like Gurley Creek, Toccoa, and Sylvan. But you may wonder—what about all those creeks and streams flowing down from the mountains with no trail in sight? There must be waterfalls on some of those as well. If you study a topo map, sometimes you'll see the word "falls" just plopped down on an obscure creek. Or looking more closely, you might notice a stream crossing a tight bunch of contour lines signifying vertical terrain. Is there a waterfall there? How do you get to those?

The fact is, there are many, many waterfalls in the mountains that few folks will ever see. They're just plain too hard to get to. The uppermost waterfall on Blood Mountain Creek is that kind of waterfall. Think of this hike as a sample "waterfall hunt." Or you may actually see it as a deterrent to waterfall hunting. There can be good reasons to stick to the beaten track.

To see this waterfall, you must be willing to venture well off the established trail, get scratched up by brambles, slog through a boulder field, and descend through a "hell." Where you leave the trail, the creek is little more than a trickle through a jumble of boulders. From here it's tough going to the top of the falls, where you can see a 30-foot slide followed by a 20-foot drop. If you made it down this far, you did well. The main falls is still below, viewable only from the bottom, looking up.

Head into the woods away from the creek in either direction, and work your way around and down to the bottom, staying well away from the waterfall. On the left you have to angle down through a laurel slick, sometimes referred to as a "hell." On the far right, it's steep woods. Do not try to climb down any boulders. They lead to a dangerous spot in the middle of the waterfall.

At the bottom you'll see two distinctly different waterfalls side by side. One drops over a cliff, the other slides down a massive rock face and they meet at the bottom. If you actually made it this far, you get a triple gold star, the highest in this book!

Whether or not you venture down to the bottom of the waterfall, this makes a superb hike around and over the very top of Blood Mountain. Wildflowers abound on the southern slope of the mountain, and the views from the top are amazing. Hike here on a clear winter day, and you can make out the Atlanta skyline 75 miles to the south. Why is it called Blood Mountain? The real reason has to do with Native American wars, but trip on those rocks coming down, and you'll swear that some bloody Appalachian Trail hikers coined the name.

SHANTY BRANCH FALLS
Class: Tiered Height: 30 ft Rating: Fair

Blood Mountain Loop (cont.)

Getting to the Trailhead

From Neels Gap north of Dahlonega on US 19/129, drive 0.6 mile north to the Byron Herbert Reece trailhead on the left.

GPS Coordinates

N 34° 44.51' W 83° 55.37'

★ =Start

Hiking Directions

Begin Walk up Byron Herbert Reece trail.

Mile 0.4 At the first set of switchbacks you'll find a cascading 30-foot waterfall on Shanty Branch. It's just off the left side of the trail through the boulders.

Mile 0.8 Cross the Appalachian Trail onto Freeman Trail.

Mile 2.1 Pay close attention here. You'll cross an upper prong of Blood Mountain Creek. There may just be a trickle of water (if it's bone dry, don't bother with this bushwhack; stay on the trail). Turn left into the woods and follow the streambed down the mountain. It's a very rough scramble through rhodo, briars, and boulders.

Mile 2.4 Brink of the falls. To reach the bottom, you'll need to circle way around one side or the other. Don't even think about scaling down any of the rocks. Although it's rough going, it's safer to stick to the woods and laurel thickets on the far sides. This is an interesting place, with slides and sheer drops forming twin waterfalls from two different prongs of Blood Mountain Creek that drop 100 feet. Try to return to Freeman Trail

Bonus Falls

TRAHLYTA FALLS
Class: Tiered Height: 80 ft Rating: Good

This waterfall is located on Wolf Creek as it flows out of Lake Trahlyta at Vogel State Park. From the Byron Reece Trailhead for Blood Mountain, drive north on US 19/129 for 2.3 miles to the state park. View the falls from a pulloff just down the road from the park entrance, or walk the lake trail within the state park down to the observation platform below the falls.

exactly the way you came (it's easy to miss it in all those boulders) and turn left to continue the loop.

Mile 3.4 Turn right on the AT.

Mile 3.8 Slaughter Creek Trail enters from the left. Stay on AT.

Mile 4.2 Duncan Ridge Trail enters from the left. Stay on AT.

Mile 4.7 Top of Blood Mountain. There's a stone shelter here as well as some great vantage points from the boulders above.

Mile 6.2 Turn left on Byron Herbert Reece Trail.

Mile 7.0 Finish.

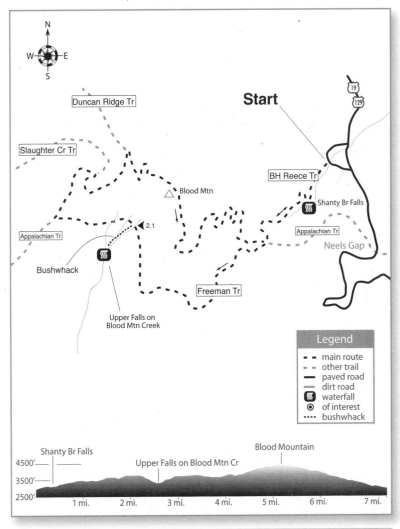

Desoto Falls Trail

Hike Distance:	2.5 miles
Type of Hike:	T-shape
Number of Falls:	2+
Hiking Time:	2 hours
Dry Feet:	Yes
Start Elevation:	2,088 ft
Total Ascent:	415 ft
Land Manager:	USFS
Fee:	$3

UPPER FALLS AT DESOTO FALLS SCENIC AREA
Class: Tiered Height: 100 ft Rating: Excellent

According to local legend, Desoto Falls Scenic Area got its name because at some point many years ago, a piece of armor believed to be from the 1540 Hernando DeSoto expedition was found at the base of one of the waterfalls.

Of all the early explorers of what is now the southeastern United States perhaps none has more places named for him than Hernando DeSoto. There is the town of DeSoto in Georgia, a county in Florida, a state park in Alabama, a bridge in Tennessee, another county in Mississippi, and a parish in Louisiana. The explorer really got around. One story even says he built the stone wall on Fort Mountain that gives the mountain its name. Legend or not, DeSoto's travels were all because of gold—or at least for old Hernado, a quest for gold. He searched for years but never found any.

You probably won't find any gold here either—or any armor—but you *will* find two easily accessible waterfalls on a frequently used and well-maintained trail. Expect to see other hikers here. The trails are not difficult; there are even benches placed along the way if you need a place to stop and rest.

The hike to the lower falls is the shortest, but getting to the viewing platform requires walking up a steep hill. Here you'll find a 40-foot-high waterfall that drops over several tiers. About 50 yards below it is another 15-foot-high drop into a pool that you can see from the trail above but cannot get to for a closer look.

The distance to the upper falls is somewhat longer, but the trail is less demanding. The waterfall itself is much higher, dropping 100 feet over multiple tiers. Along the way to the upper falls, be on the lookout for wildflowers

HIDDEN FALLS BELOW LOWER FALLS
Class: Block Height: 15 ft Rating: Fair

between the trail and Frogtown Creek. Showy orchis, violets, and trillium abound in April and May. Also keep your eyes peeled for a spring on the slope side of the trail. Stones are still neatly stacked to wall it off. Years ago, someone must have lived in the area and used the spring as a source of water. Perhaps DeSoto and his men stopped here for a drink, set down a piece of armor, and began a legend.

LOWER FALLS AT DESOTO FALLS SCENIC AREA
Class: Tiered Height: 40 ft Rating: Good

Desoto Falls Trail (cont.)

Getting to the Trailhead

From Dahlonega, drive north to Turners Corner on US 19. Continue another 5.0 miles north on US 19/129 to the Desoto Falls Scenic Area. It's on the left side of the road before you reach Neels Gap. Park in the day-use parking lot.

GPS Coordinates

N 34° 42.39' W 83° 54.92'

Hiking Directions

Begin From the day-use area, follow the trail down through the picnic area and around the lower edge of the campground. Cross the footbridge and turn left toward the lower falls.

Mile 0.4 Viewing platform for the lower falls. This a 40-foot tiered drop. Downstream about 50 yards is another 15-foot drop which you can see from the trail above. Turn back here and re-trace your steps to the main trail.

Mile 0.7 Back at the footbridge, continue straight on the trail which follows Frogtown Creek, heading upstream.

Mile 1.4 Cross a branch of Frogtown Creek on a footbridge, then turn left toward the upper falls.

Mile 1.5 Viewing platform for the upper falls. This is a much higher, 100-foot multi-tiered drop. From here, turn around and head back to the trailhead the way you came.

Mile 2.3 Turn left to cross over the footbridge.

Mile 2.5 Finish.

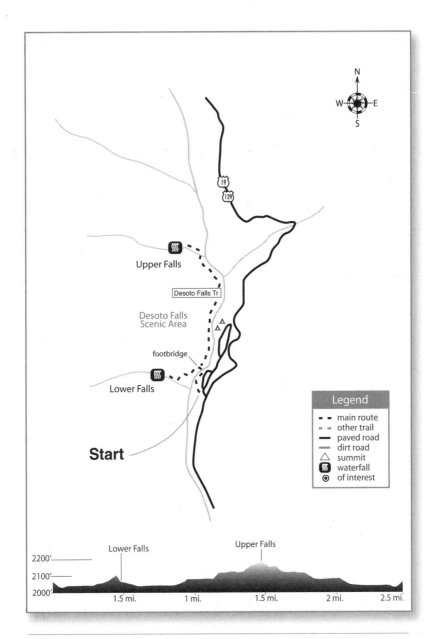

Upper Falls

Desoto Falls Tr

Desoto Falls
Scenic Area

footbridge

Lower Falls

Start

2200'
2100'
2000'

Lower Falls

Upper Falls

1.5 mi.   1 mi.   1.5 mi.   2 mi.   2.5 mi.

Little Ridge Creek Falls

Hike Distance:	1.5 miles
Type of Hike:	Out & Back
Number of Falls:	4
Hiking Time:	2 hours
Dry Feet:	No
Start Elevation:	1,888 ft
Total Ascent:	380 ft
Land Manager:	USFS
Fee:	None

SECOND FALLS ON LITTLE RIDGE CREEK
Class: Fan Height: 70 ft Rating: Excellent

It's a treat. What else could you call a relatively short hike to four very nice waterfalls—all very near to each other? This one takes you up an old roadbed that eventually turns into an unmarked path. The path leads to the various falls.

Boggs Creek tumbles down out of the Raven Cliffs Wilderness Area. High above, following the crest of the Blue Ridge Valley Divide, is the Appalachian Trail. Hikers walking on the trail up there could not imagine you hopping around on the creeks down here. Two mountain ridges over, across Cowrock Mountain and Wildcat Mountain, are the famous Raven Cliffs that give the wilderness area its name. That's remote territory. This is less so, but it feels remote just the same.

Driving to the trailhead you'll pass through the Boggs Creek Recreation Area. The name makes it sound like a place with tennis courts and a pool, but "recreation area" means something different in the national forest. Expect to find dispersed camping spots and pit toilets—that's about it. The sites are level and quite pleasant, right beside Boggs

Creek. Many folks come to camp here and fish in the creek. Others just like to hang out in the cool shade. And of course others come to hike to the waterfalls here and on Cowrock Creek, the next stream up the road.

Little Ridge Creek flows into Boggs Creek. You'll park and start the hike just before the road fords Little Ridge Creek. Look for a dirt mound blocking an old roadbed right beside the stream. That roadbed is your trail.

The first waterfall you'll come to is the smallest. With five tiers and a drop of 20 feet, it rates a fair, mainly whetting your appetite for the three waterfalls that follow. In quick succession the stream

THIRD FALLS ON LITTLE RIDGE CREEK
Class: Tiered Height: 40 ft Rating: Good

drops 15, then 40, then 70 feet over a series of sluices, slides, fans, and tiers. Of course you'll come to them from the bottom up, which saves the smallest—but most interesting one of these three—for last. At the final falls, the creek folds on itself so it can fit through a narrow cleft between large boulders.

While you're in the neighborhood, be sure to hike on up and see if you can find Cowrock Creek Falls (p. 194).

FIRST FALLS ON LITTLE RIDGE CREEK
Class: Tiered Height: 20 ft Rating: Fair

Little Ridge Creek Falls (cont.)

Getting to the Trailhead

From Dahlonega, go north on US 19 to Turners Corner, then take US 19/129 for 1.5 miles and turn right into the Boggs Creek Recreation Area. Continue another 1.9 miles to the first creek ford. Park just before the ford.

GPS Coordinates

N 34° 41.99' W 83° 53.18'

4TH FALLS ON LITTLE RIDGE CREEK
Class: Sluice Height: 15 ft Rating: Good

Mile 0.6 Top of second falls, a 30-foot slide leading into a 40-foot drop.

Mile 0.7 Third falls, a double-tiered slide that drops 40 feet, fanning out at the bottom.

Mile 0.75 Just beyond the third falls is the fourth falls. Here the water channels down through a very tight sluice/cleft in the rocks while dropping 15 feet—an impressive sight. Return from here the way you came in.

Mile 1.5 Finish.

Hiking Directions

Begin Walk over the dirt mound and up the well-defined but unmarked trail beside Little Ridge Creek.

Mile 0.2 Hop across a small feeder stream, go a little farther and then ford the creek. You should see a less well-defined path that leads up a very old roadbed. Follow that path.

Mile 0.5 The first waterfall is on your left, a quintuple-tiered cascade that drops 20 feet over a 30-foot stretch.

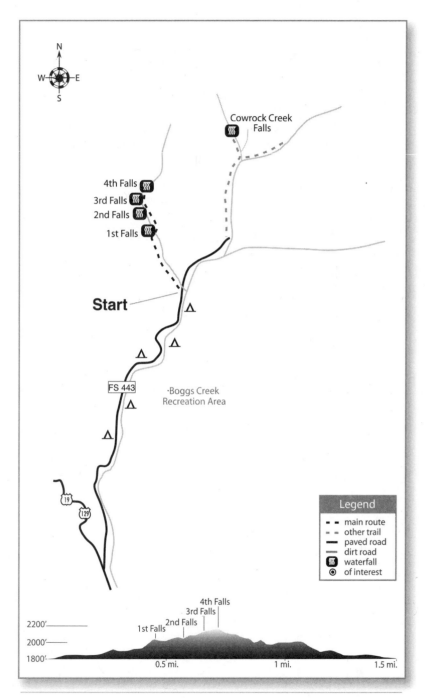

Cowrock Creek
Falls

4th Falls
3rd Falls
2nd Falls
1st Falls

Start

FS 443

·Boggs Creek
Recreation Area

19
129

Legend

- - main route
- - other trail
— paved road
— dirt road
waterfall
◉ of interest

4th Falls
3rd Falls
2nd Falls
1st Falls

2200'
2000'
1800'

0.5 mi.   1 mi.   1.5 mi.

Cowrock Creek Falls

Hike Distance:	1.5 miles
Type of Hike:	Out & Back
Number of Falls:	2
Hiking Time:	2 hours
Dry Feet:	No
Start Elevation:	1,900 ft
Total Ascent:	250 ft
Land Manager:	USFS
Fee:	None

COWROCK CREEK FALLS
Class: Slide Height: 50 ft Rating: Good

This is the you-get-the-bronze-star-if-you-find-it waterfall, so pay close attention to the directions.

Getting to the Trailhead

From Dahlonega, go north on US 19 to Turners Corner. Take US 19/129 for 1.5 miles and turn right into the Boggs Creek Recreation Area. Continue another 2.2 miles to the end of the road. **Caution**: Creek ford.

GPS Coordinates
N 34° 42.18′ W 83° 52.94′

Hiking Directions

Begin Walk over the dirt mound and up the well-defined but unmarked trail.

Mile 0.5 Cross a small stream. Go 25 paces and turn left on a faint trail that follows the stream you just crossed.

Mile 0.6 The stream forks here. You can take the right fork 0.1 mile up to a small 15-foot waterfall which is on the feeder stream in front of you. Take the left fork by crossing the feeder stream,

then aiming just to the left and below a rhodo-covered boulder. This leads to Cowrock Falls. First follow the faint roadbed and then just walk up the creek.

Mile 0.8 Cowrock Creek Falls, a steep 50-foot-high slide where half the water runs under an overlapping rock face through a gap about 10 inches high and 4 feet deep—it looks like a sideways toaster slot. Turn back here and return to trailhead.

Mile 1.5 Finish.

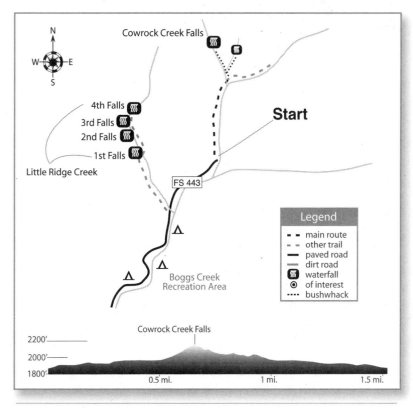

Blood Mountain Creek Falls

Hike Distance:	2 miles
Type of Hike:	Out & Back
Number of Falls:	1
Hiking Time:	2 hours
Dry Feet:	No
Start Elevation:	2,311 ft
Total Ascent:	445 ft
Land Manager:	USFS
Fee:	None

SECOND FALLS ON BLOOD MOUNTAIN CREEK
Class: Tiered Height: 80 ft Rating: Excellent

High on the side of Blood Mountain is the source of Blood Mountain Creek. If you've hiked Blood Mountain Loop (p. 182), you've seen its headwaters way up there—barely a trickle among a heap of boulders. Of the four waterfalls on Blood Mountain Creek, the first and most remote is nearly impossible to get to. This hike leads you to the second falls which is much easier to find, and the hike to it is pleasant.

Starting out on a gated forest road, you'll walk along the border of the Blood Mountain Wilderness Area down to a wildlife field and the banks of Blood Mountain Creek. If you're quiet on the way down, you might spot a deer or a flock of turkey feeding in the field. Once at the creek, it's amazing to see how much water a stream can pick up in just a few miles. What was a mere trickle high up on the mountain is now a full-fledged creek.

At the field, turn upstream and follow the unmarked path. It's been used frequently enough to make for easy going. You're now well within the Wilderness Area and heading into what's known as Blood Mountain

Cove. Soon after reaching a campsite, you'll start to hear the roar of the falls just ahead. At its base, cross over to the other side of the creek for the best view.

As you'll see, the waterfall drops over two tiers and ends on a big slab slide. For a better view, you can scramble up through the open woods to several boulder cliffs above and to the left of the falls.

Two Bonus Falls on Blood Mountain Creek

THIRD FALLS (THIRD TIER) Class: Tiered
Height: 120 ft Rating: Excellent

of a pool and creates a strong draft. Seen from above, this falls looks like a exclamation point. Continue on up the goatpath, and above the pool you'll see three more tiers forming sluices and slides. The total drop is 120 feet.

Back at the campsite, walk a short distance up the campsite side of the creek to access the fourth and final waterfall on Blood Mountain Creek before it enters Dicks Creek just below the bridge. It's a 25-foot, tiered rock jumble drop rating fair to good, depending on the water level.

Driving to the trailhead on FS 34 you'll pass near two more waterfalls on Blood Mountain Creek. At mile 4.6 from US 19 you'll cross a low-water bridge. Park at the campsite just before the bridge on the right. To access the upper falls (actually the third falls on Blood Mountain Creek), walk up the well-used goatpath on the left side of the creek, opposite the campsite. About 0.2 mile up the trail, you'll find a huge waterfall with four distinct tiers. The fourth and lowest tier sluices into a deep green bowl

THIRD FALLS (FOURTH TIER) Class: Tiered
Height: 120 ft Rating: Excellent

Blood Mountain Creek Falls (cont.)

Getting to the Trailhead

Drive 12.5 miles north on US 19, or drive 0.5 mile south of the junction of US 19 and US 129 (Turners Corner). Turn onto Dicks Creek Road. Where the pavement ends, the road becomes FS 34. You'll drive past several waterfalls on Dicks Creek, up through the Dicks Creek Dispersed Camping Area, past the trailhead for Crow Mountain Creek Falls, past the trail to the bonus lower falls on Blood Mountain Creek, and past another bonus falls on Dicks Creek—for a total of 6.0 miles to a gate marking the end of the road at the boundary for the Blood Mountain Wilderness Area. **Caution:** Creek fords on FS 34.

GPS Coordinates

N 34° 42.38′ W 83° 57.29′

Hiking Directions

Begin Walk around the gate and down the roadbed.

Mile 0.3 Reach a wildlife field. Turn left on the unmarked trail heading upstream alongside Blood Mountain Creek.

Mile 1.0 Reach the base of the waterfall. It's hard to see much from this side, so ford the creek for a better view. You'll see a two-tiered fan falling into a slide, followed by a sluice. It drops a total of 80 feet. Return the way you came.

Mile 2.0 Finish.

Bonus Falls

UPPER FALLS ON DICKS CREEK
Class: Tiered Height: 20 ft Rating: Fair

This waterfall is located on Dicks Creek. You'll pass it at mile 4.9 from US 19 on your way to the trailhead. It's just off the left side of the road, 0.3 mile north of the low-water bridge across Blood Mountain Creek where the two bonus lower falls on Blood Mountain Creek are located.

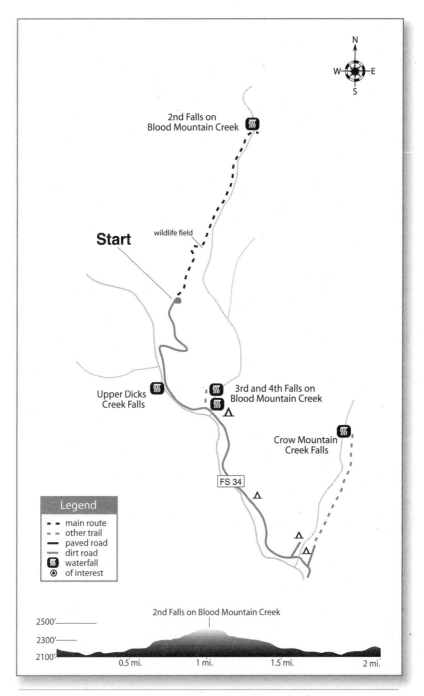

2nd Falls on
Blood Mountain Creek

wildlife field

Start

Upper Dicks
Creek Falls

3rd and 4th Falls on
Blood Mountain Creek

Crow Mountain
Creek Falls

FS 34

Legend
- - main route
- - other trail
— paved road
— dirt road
waterfall
of interest

2nd Falls on Blood Mountain Creek

2500'
2300'
2100'
0.5 mi.   1 mi.   1.5 mi.   2 mi.

Crow Mountain Creek Falls

Hike Distance:	1.8 miles
Type of Hike:	Out & Back
Number of Falls:	1
Hiking Time:	2 hours
Dry Feet:	Maybe
Start Elevation:	1,785 ft
Total Ascent:	600 ft
Land Manager:	USFS
Fee:	None

MIDDLE TIERS OF CROW MOUNTAIN CREEK FALLS
Class: Tiered Height: 150 ft Rating: Excellent

When walking up to most waterfalls, you usually have some sense that you're getting close to something special. You may see glimpses of whitewater ahead of time, or you may hear an increasingly loud roar. This is not the case with the waterfall on Crow Mountain Creek. An old roadbed trail leads you silently up the mountainside and all of a sudden, wow!—there it is! You're at the top of it before you know it.

Although you start the hike to Crow Mountain Creek Falls from below it, you actually access the waterfall from above. The trail circles wide around the falls on the way to the top. Once there, you see only the top tier, with the rest of the waterfall cascading off the side of the mountain.

If you opt to stay on the trail, you won't see very much of the waterfall at all, so here's what you need to do. Once you've had a good look around at the top, go back down the trail about 50 yards, then turn right off the trail and head down into the woods at an angle aiming back toward the lower part of the falls. In this way you'll be able to walk down alongside the different tiers and get a good view of many of them. Going down (and eventually back up) is not too steep, and the woods are pleasantly open, making for fair walking. You'll find this waterfall crashes down the mountain in a series of giant, near-vertical slides, with a few sluices and ledges thrown in. The tallest single slide is around 30 feet high, while the entire waterfall drops 150 feet. Below many of the tiers there's plenty of room for crossing back and forth or standing in the middle to get a photo without fear of tumbling over the next drop. Go down as far as you like, but keep in mind you'll have to come back up to the trail at some point for your return hike.

UPPER TIER OF CROW MOUNTAIN CREEK FALLS
Class: Tiered Height: 150 ft Rating: Excellent

Driving to the trailhead you'll see that the Dicks Creek watershed is a popular place. In the first mile and half you'll pass through an area of vacation homes—at least one with its own private, deluxe waterfall viewing platform. Beyond the houses, the road enters the national forest. It turns to gravel and soon passes Dicks Creek Falls, which is now so popular it has its own parking lot. Lots of folks hang out here on hot summer days. Nearer the trailhead you'll enter a dispersed camping area. Expect to see all kinds of folks camping by the roadside.

MIDDLE TIER OF CROW MOUNTAIN CREEK FALLS
Class: Tiered Height: 150 ft Rating: Excellent

Crow Mountain Creek Falls (cont.)

Getting to the Trailhead

Drive 12.5 miles north of Dahlonega on US 19 *or* 0.5 mile south of the junction of US 19 and US 129 (Turners Corner). Turn onto Dicks Creek Road. Where the pavement ends, the road becomes FS 34. Continue past several waterfalls on Dicks Creek and up through the Dicks Creek Dispersed Camping Area, for a total of 3.6 miles, to a ford across Crow Mountain Creek. Just before the ford, a road turns right into a campsite. Park at the campsite.

GPS Coordinates
N 34° 41.23' W 83° 56.62'

Hiking Directions

Begin The trail is an old roadbed that begins by paralleling the short campsite road on which you just drove in. Look for the dirt berm just off FS 34 and start walking there. The roadbed is so old and sunken, it's like walking up a stone-lined

bobsled run. You'll follow this roadbed all the way to the falls.

Mile 0.8 Top of Crow Mountain Creek Falls—wow! Head back down the trail about 50 yards and enter the woods to walk down alongside the falls for views of the different tiers. It's the only way to see all of the falls, and it's not too steep. When you're ready, return the way you came.

Mile 1.8 Finish.

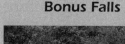
Bonus Falls

DICKS CREEK FALLS
Class: Block Height: 35 ft Rating: Good

On the way to the trailhead you'll pass a waterfall on Dicks Creek located on private land. Dicks Creek Falls is the second waterfall. You'll find it just off the left side of the road at mile 2.8 after you leave US 19. Drive just past it and park in the falls parking lot on the right.

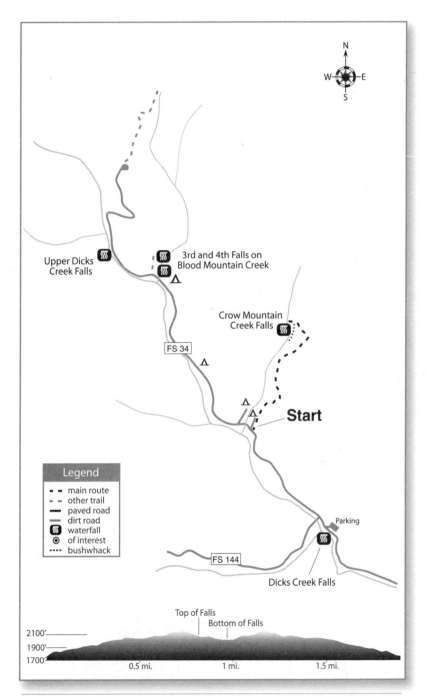

Upper Dicks
Creek Falls

3rd and 4th Falls on
Blood Mountain Creek

Crow Mountain
Creek Falls

FS 34

Start

Legend

- main route
- other trail
- paved road
- dirt road
- waterfall
- of interest
- bushwhack

Parking

FS 144

Dicks Creek Falls

Top of Falls
Bottom of Falls

2100'
1900'
1700'

0.5 mi.   1 mi.   1.5 mi.

Dockery Lake Trail

Hike Distance:	4.8 miles
Type of Hike:	Out & Back
Number of Falls:	5
Hiking Time:	Half day
Dry Feet:	No
Start Elevation:	2,464 ft
Total Ascent:	1,322 ft
Land Manager:	USFS
Fee:	None

MARTHA FALLS ON PIGEON ROOST CREEK
Class: Tiered Height: 200 ft Rating: Excellent

The gold star. Yep, this is it. You'll have the opportunity to see no fewer than five waterfalls on this hike. That is, if you actually happen to find Martha Falls on Pigeon Roost Creek. If you do, you'll get that gold star. Really, it's not that hard. It's just a matter of studying the map and directions, *and* paying attention while you're on the trail. Crossing your fingers and turning around three times with your eyes closed won't hurt either.

The greater portion of this hike follows a beautiful trail. After leaving Dockery Lake, you'll head into the Blood Mountain Wilderness. The trail

SPILLWAY FALLS ON DOCKERY CREEK
Class: Horsetail Height: 15 ft Rating: Fair

BOTTOM OF PIGEON ROOST CREEK FALLS
Class: Tiered Height: 200 ft Rating: Excellent

skirts a high ridge overlooking the Waters Creek watershed before dropping down to parallel Pigeon Roost Creek. At this point, once near the creek, you could head straight over to it, turn upstream, and eventually come to Martha Falls. But that difficult walk might take all day. On this route you'll follow the established trail as far as possible, then skip over the ridge to the falls. Whichever way you get there, finding Martha Falls is well worth the effort. Cascading 200 feet down the side of the mountain, it's an amazing sight.

On the hike in, just after leaving the lake, you'll most likely hear Dockery Creek roaring well below the trail. On your return trip, check out the cause of all this noise and you'll be in for a pleasant surprise. There's more to see here.

Immediately below Dockery Lake, Dockery Creek begins a serious plunge down the mountain to join Waters Creek far below. First there is a horsetail plunge just below the spillway. A little farther down, the creek forms a series of constricted sluices. It's as if the water flows through a solid stone ditch, creating a ribbon of white. You can view it all from the right side of the creek by following a goatpath downstream through the rhododendron thicket.

Below the sluices, Dockery Creek makes its final plunge, dropping 100 feet over a cliff and disappearing from view.

MIDDLE FALLS ON DOCKERY CREEK
Class: Sluice Height: 15 ft Rating: Fair

Dockery Lake Trail (cont.)

Getting to the Trailhead

Take GA 60 north from Dahlonega for 15.0 miles and turn right into Dockery Lake Recreation Area. Continue down to the trailhead parking area near the lake.

GPS Coordinates

N 34° 40.39' W 83° 58.62'

UPPER FALLS ON DOCKERY CREEK
Class: Sluice Height: 12 ft Rating: Fair

over the old wall into the woods. Now walk at a right angle to the trail, over the rise, and down toward Pigeon Roost Creek. If the stars have lined up correctly, you hold your teeth right, and

Hiking Directions

Begin Walk down onto the Dockery Lake Trail and head around the left side of the lake.

Mile 0.3 The dam will be just to your right. Bear left, following the sign indicating this trail leads to the Appalachian Trail. You can hear Dockery Creek crashing down below. You'll check out the source of that noise later.

Mile 2.0 Pay close attention here. The trail will have been following an old roadbed lined with moss-covered stones. You'll cross two small streams within 0.2 mile. After crossing the second one, step off 100 paces and turn right off the trail and

LOWER FALLS ON DOCKERY CREEK
Class: Horsetail Height: 100 ft Rating: Excellent

you did not cheat on your taxes, you should see the waterfall right ahead of you. Good luck. After viewing the falls (or wandering around aimlessly), return the way you came on Dockery Lake Trail.

Mile 4.5 Just before the dam to Dockery Lake, turn to the left down off the trail. Immediately you'll see a 15-foot waterfall just below the spillway. Cross the creek here and look for the faint goatpath heading down alongside Dockery Creek. Just

downstream is a series of three waterfalls. The first two drop 12 feet and 15 feet through a very tight sluice area. The creek then careens off the side of the mountain in a 100-foot horsetail plunge. Return from here past the dam, around the lake, and back to the trailhead.

Mile 4.8 Finish.

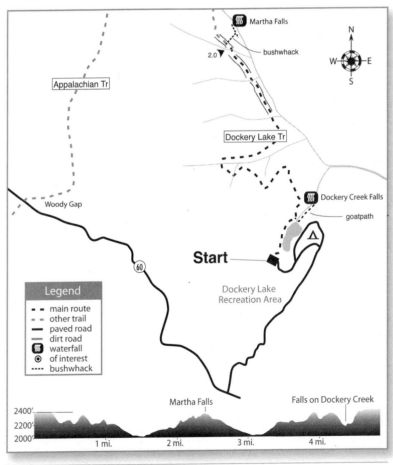

Northeast Corner

FOURTH FALLS ON MOCCASIN CREEK

NORTHEAST CORNER ROAD MAP WITH FALLS

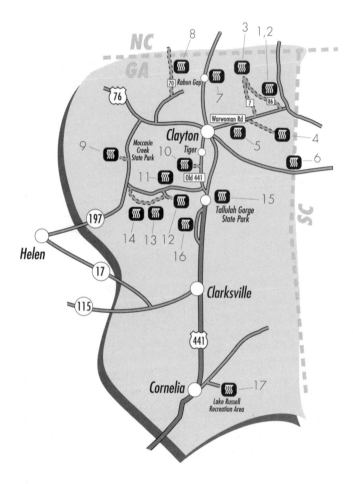

1. Big Creek Circuit
2. Three Forks East
3. Holcomb Creek Trail
4. Dicks Creek Falls Trail
5. Warwoman Dell–Bartram Trail
6. Bull Sluice
7. Darnell Creek Falls
8. Tate City
9. Hemlock Falls Trail
10. Stonewall Falls
11. Angel Falls Trail
12. Minnehaha Falls Trail
13. Bad Branch Falls
14. Crow Creek Falls
15. Tallulah Gorge Scramble
16. Panther Creek Trail
17. Sourwood Trail

The northeastern corner of Georgia is especially waterfall-rich. In this section you'll find hikes leading to 60 waterfalls, all on Georgia's public lands. Tucked away and hidden in the folds of the hills, there are even more. If you count those on private property, the number jumps well above 100.

This abundance of waterfalls is due to the lay of the land. The Georgia–South Carolina border is formed by the Chattooga River, the product of a major watershed. The Chattooga flows into Lake Tugaloo, becomes the Savannah River, and empties into the Atlantic Ocean. In so doing it drains the waters of half of two states like a giant siphon. Every river and creek in this section eventually joins the Chattooga, and in their rush to do so, waterfall after waterfall is formed.

This area marks the edge of the Southern Blue Ridge Province, where the foothills rise up to form the great chain of the Appalachian Mountains. The official name of this gargantuan geological formation is the Blue Ridge Escarpment. In South Carolina the Cherokee Indians called it the Blue Wall, and from a distance, that's exactly what it looks like in Georgia as well. The elevation change is dramatic—and so are the waterfalls you find here.

As you flip through the pages of this section, you'll see quite a variety of hikes to choose from. Some are short and relatively easy, so you can take two or more simple walks in a day's outing. Others are extreme day hikes that will push both your physical endurance and route-finding abilities to their limits. This section is also where you'll find Minnehaha Falls. Every state seems to have one, and this is Georgia's.

DICKS CREEK LEDGE

Big Creek Circuit

Hike Distance:	9 miles
Type of Hike:	Lollipop
Number of Falls:	5
Hiking Time:	Full day
Dry Feet:	No
Start Elevation:	2,307 ft
Total Ascent:	2,545 ft
Land Manager:	USFS
Fee:	None

THIRD FALLS ON BIG CREEK
Class: Tiered Height: 80 feet Rating: Excellent

This is one of the most difficult hikes in the book. It's not so much the elevation gain, although there's plenty of that. What makes it hard is that, to see three of the waterfalls on Big Creek, you have to rely on what in this book is known as a "goatpath." These trails are not actually used by goats, but created by humans who want to see the falls. With no established trail available, people make a track by repeated bushwhacking, following the path of least resistance. In this case the "trail" that's been created is fairly visible and not difficult to find. However, it crosses through some rugged terrain, and at times it seems to barely cling to the mountainside. You

SINGLEYS FALLS ON OVERFLOW CREEK
Class: Sluice Height: 20 ft Rating: Good

get two gold stars if you make it to all five falls.

The waterfalls on Big Creek are all stunning, and so is Singleys Falls on Overflow Creek. After making a side trip to view Singleys, you'll work your way down to Three Forks. This is where Big, Overflow, and Holcomb Creeks come together to form the West Fork of the Chattooga River, and it's a special place. Right at the junction, both Holcomb and Big Creek crash into the West Fork as waterfalls.

Four waterfalls on Big Creek are listed on this hike. There may be even more; from the goatpath high above the creek, you can hear a lot of loud crashing down below. But the terrain is so rugged and precipitous, we may never know what's down there. Getting to the second, third, and fourth falls is difficult enough.

How do you do it? If you stick to the well-defined path, you should be fine. Use your ears as well as your eyes. If you hear a loud crashing waterfall noise and you see a path leading in that direction, go that way. If the path fades out or you find yourself staring into an abyss, get back to the main goatpath and continue working your way upstream.

First Falls on Big Creek at Three Forks
Class: Slide Height: 30 ft Rating: Good

Allow plenty of time for this hike. There are good lunch spots on the boulders just below Singleys Falls or at Three Forks. Due to the scrambling you'll do along Big Creek, avoid this hike on a rainy day, when the ground will be slippery.

Second Falls on Big Creek
Class: Horsetail Height: 25 ft Rating: Good

Big Creek Circuit (cont.)

Getting to the Trailhead

From Clayton, take Warwoman Road 14.0 miles to its end at GA 28. Turn left and drive 4.4 miles. Park at the pullout on the left, 0.2 mile past the bridge over Big Creek.

GPS Coordinates

N 34° 59.05′ W 83° 11.63′

Hiking Directions

Begin Walk down the old roadbed and ford Talley Mill Creek.

Mile 1.4 The trail forks here on the spine of the ridge. Turn right.

Mile 2.3 A trail exits to the right

FOURTH FALLS ON BIG CREEK
Class: Sluice Height: 40 ft Rating: Excellent

here over two dirt mounds. Go straight over the single mound.

Mile 2.5 The trail forks here at a dirt mound with a swampy puddle in front of it. Turn right.

Mile 3.0 Turn hard left at the fork.

Mile 3.1 Turn right off the old road-bed down the goatpath to Singleys Falls. You can hear it as you go.

Mile 3.2 Singleys Falls on Overflow Creek. After exploring around here, return the way you came back to mile 2.5.

Mile 4.0 Turn right at the swampy puddle and go around the dirt mound.

Mile 5.0 Turn right at the T-intersection down the steep hill to Three Forks.

Mile 5.1 Three Forks. The first falls on Big Creek is just ahead of you. You can't see it from this vantage point, but there is another waterfall just downstream where Holcomb Creek enters Three Forks. It's hidden behind a rock. Return to the T-intersection and follow the goatpath that parallels Big Creek, heading upstream.

Mile 5.5 There is a split in the goatpath here. Head to the right, steeply downhill.

Mile 5.6 You should now be at the bottom of the second falls on Big Creek, a 25-foot-high crashing horsetail with a big pool at the bottom. From here, go back up to your last turn and then go right to continue following the goatpath on the contour line well above Big Creek.

Mile 5.9 The goatpath has ended

and you should be following an old roadbed. A faint path turns off to the right here and leads to the base of the third falls. If you miss it, continue on the old road; it circles around and meets Big Creek, where you can turn back to the right to access the falls from the top.

Mile 6.0 Third falls on Big Creek. This monster has four tiers and drops 80 feet. From the top of this falls, continue on the path just beside the now quiet creek. Eventually you'll begin a slow ascent up the hillside.

Mile 6.9 You're back at mile 1.4. Turn right toward the trailhead.

Mile 7.6 Just past the last dirt mound (the first one you got to on your way in), turn right off the road and scramble down the very steep goatpath. You should hear the falls below. The goatpath leads down between two cliffs where you'll need to angle left, directly below the left cliff. Go past it, and then angle right down to the falls. You should see a 40-foot drop into a very tight, cliff-sided mini-gorge. Return to the road the way you came down and turn right to retrace your steps to the trailhead.

Mile 9.0 Finish.

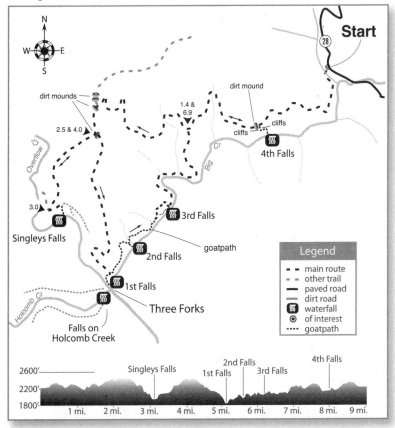

Three Forks East

Hike Distance:	3.8 mile
Type of Hike:	Out & Back
Number of Falls:	7
Hiking Time:	Half day
Dry Feet:	No
Start Elevation:	2,357 ft
Total Ascent:	1,000 ft
Land Manager:	USFS
Fee:	None

UPPER FALLS ON HOLCOMB CREEK
Class: Sluice Height: 30 ft Rating: Good

Three Forks, that area where Overflow Creek, Big Creek, and Holcomb Creek come together to form the West Fork of the Chattooga River, has got to be one of the most difficult places to get to in the entire northeastern corner of Georgia. Even the Three Forks Trail stops 0.2 mile short of the location from which it takes its name; it makes you wonder why it was named Three Forks Trail in the first place. Of course, if you're an expert whitewater kayaker, you could just paddle down Overflow Creek to the confluence. However, take one look at the extreme rapids and waterfalls along that stretch, and you can see there won't be too many folks getting there that way. You can get there hiking, but whether you come in from the north via Big Creek Circuit (p. 212) or from the south as described here, it is steep, rugged terrain. These two routes are your only access options on foot. Nevertheless, once you do arrive, you'll see it is a very special place.

It seems that whenever three streams come together in one place, the area is called Three Forks. As the hike name says, this is the eastern Three

Forks route. West of here, over near Springer Mountain and the southern terminus of the Appalachian Trail, is another area with the same name. If you're looking for that hike and destination, see p. 108.

On this route, you'll begin high, off a lonely forest road at John Teague Gap. The trail quickly descends into the upper West Fork of the Chattooga River watershed. You will have crossed over the West Fork on your drive to the trailhead. A good, well-marked trail brings you down to Holcomb Creek and your first waterfall—a 30-foot sluice that sends the water barreling down through a long, pothole-filled crevice. It's the begin-

BOTTOM FALLS IN HOLCOMB CREEK GORGE
Class: Sluice Height: 30 ft Rating: Good

ning of a series of similar drops that continue through a 0.2-mile mini-gorge all the way to Three Forks. No wonder the trail stops here. To get to the actual Three Forks, you need to traverse above that gorge. There is a goatpath option on either side of Holcomb Creek. The one on the far left side is strongly recommended; it's far safer and the least difficult. Just hope Holcomb Creek is not running too high to cross.

Once at Three Forks you can check out the waterfalls where Big Creek and Holcomb Creek make a final plunge into the river and, if the water is not too high, do a rockhopping bushwhack up to the lower falls on Overflow Creek. Enjoy.

LOWER FALLS ON HOLCOMB CREEK
Class: Block Height: 10 ft Rating: Fair

Three Forks East (cont.)

Getting to the Trailhead

From Clayton, take Warwoman Road 13.8 miles and turn left on Overflow Creek Road (FS 86). Continue 4.0 miles to the trailhead at John Teague Gap.

GPS Coordinates

N 34° 57.73' W 83° 13.72'

LOWER FALLS ON OVERFLOW CREEK
Class: Tiered Height: 15 ft Rating: Fair

Hiking Directions

Begin Walk past the granite trail marker and down Three Forks Trail.

Mile 1.0 Turn left on the old woods road, continuing downhill.

Mile 1.2 Holcomb Creek. There's a big rock slab here overlooking a 30-foot slot waterfall. This is the uppermost falls you'll see on this creek. Head upstream 25 paces, under the overhanging bluff and around the big boulder. Ford the creek just above the small rapid and then angle right into the woods. You should find a well-used goatpath which parallels the mini-gorge.

Mile 1.4 Scramble down the very steep slope to Overflow Creek at Three Forks. There is a high waterfall directly across

Bonus Falls

FALLS ON LONG BRANCH
Class: Tiered Height: 30 ft Rating: Fair

Follow the old roadbed across the road from the trailhead and use your ears to find this waterfall. It's about 0.2 mile away and hidden in the rhododendron. It's a low-flow stream, so you'll need wet weather.

the river on Big Creek. Turn left and make your way upstream alongside Overflow Creek. There is no trail, but you can alternately weave through the rhodo and rockhop along the shore.

Mile 1.9 Reach the lower falls on Overflow Creek. Return to Three Forks.

Mile 2.4 Back at Three Forks, check out the pretty 10-foot falls

dropping directly into the West Fork. You may need to ford Holcomb Creek to get the best view. Also check out the 30-foot sluice falls just upstream on Holcomb Creek. There are two more like it within the mini-gorge itself but they are not worth a possible fall from the extreme goatpath shown on the map. From here, retrace your route back to the trailhead.

Mile 3.8 Finish.

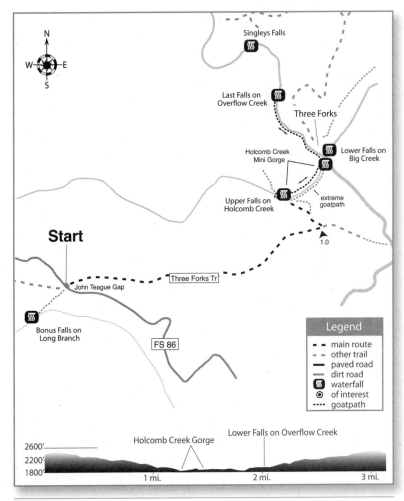

Legend
- - main route
= = other trail
— paved road
～ dirt road
🌊 waterfall
◉ of interest
···· goatpath

Holcomb Creek Trail

Hike Distance:	1.9 miles
Type of Hike:	Loop
Number of Falls:	3
Hiking Time:	2 hours
Dry Feet:	Yes
Start Elevation:	2,540 ft
Total Ascent:	580 ft
Land Manager:	USFS
Fee:	None

HOLCOMB CREEK FALLS
Class: Tiered Height: 150 ft Rating: Spectacular

Sometimes there's a waterfall so stunning that no matter how far back it is in the forest, people just seem to know about it and flock to it. The waterfalls on Holcomb Creek and Ammons Creek fit into that category. The gravel road to the trailhead is long and winding, but the hike to the falls is fairly short and relatively easy. Holcomb Creek Falls can be reached in 20 minutes or less via a well-maintained forest trail. As long as you don't mind walking up and down some gentle hills, you should have no problem with any part of this loop hike.

As with many of the more popular waterfalls in Chattahoochee National Forest, you can expect to view these falls from wooden decks and bridges. There are several good reasons for these structures. Number one, of course, is that they provide a great vantage point. Many times, to get a good view or to take a nice picture of a waterfall, you have to wade out into the creek or find purchase on a slippery boulder. With an observation deck in place, you keep your feet dry and get the best view at the same time.

AMMONS CREEK FALLS
Class: Tiered Height: 75 ft Rating: Excellent

Another obvious rationale for the decks is safety—it requires folks to observe the waterfall from a secure location. All too often someone feels the need to scale a cliff beside a waterfall, and then, unfortunately, the climber comes tumbling down. It's a hard landing *and* a hard way to learn a lesson. Stay off the steep terrain close to the falls.

The third good reason for viewing platforms is one you might not think of unless you've visited popular waterfalls without decks in place—erosion control. Whenever you put a lot of people on a soft, wet, dirt surface, the trail is going to degrade. Soil along the shore ends up washing into the creek and causing all kinds of problems with the delicate aquatic life there. What's more, it just doesn't look nice to see exposed roots hanging above the creek and deep boot prints defacing the hillsides. So if it occurs to you that a viewing platform might be marring the natural scenery, think about what the scenery might look like without the protection the platform provides.

On this hike you'll see three waterfalls on a loop of less than two miles, and almost the entire time you'll hear the sound of crashing water. Something about that noise just seems to lift your spirits.

UPPER HOLCOMB CREEK FALLS
Class: Sluice Height: 20 ft Rating: Fair

Holcomb Creek Trail (cont.)

Getting to the Trailhead

From Clayton, take Warwoman Road 10.1 miles, turn left on FS 7 (Hale Ridge Road), and drive a long, curvy, sometimes bumpy 6.6 miles to the trailhead at the intersection with FS 86. Park on the right, just before you get to the intersection.

GPS Coordinates

N 34° 58.69′ W 83° 15.99′

★ =Start

Hiking Directions

Begin Walk across FS 86 and look for the small granite boulder with the trail name etched into the rock. This marks the beginning of Holcomb Creek Trail. Head on down it.

Mile 0.3 Reach Holcomb Creek Falls. There is an observation platform/bridge here across the creek. After viewing the falls, continue along farther on Holcomb Creek Trail.

Mile 0.5 Reach Ammons Creek Falls. There is an observation platform here as well. After viewing the falls, backtrack a

very short distance and turn right to continue on Holcomb Creek Trail. The turn onto this part of the trail may be hard to see. You'll soon begin to climb up and around Holcomb Creek Falls. You can hear it crashing over to your left.

Mile 1.1 The trail leads up past an upper sluice/slide waterfall 20 feet high on Holcomb Creek. After viewing the falls, continue on Holcomb Creek Trail.

Mile 1.3 Holcomb Creek Trail ends on FS 86 (Holcomb Creek Road). Turn left and walk the road back to the trailhead.

Mile 1.9 Finish.

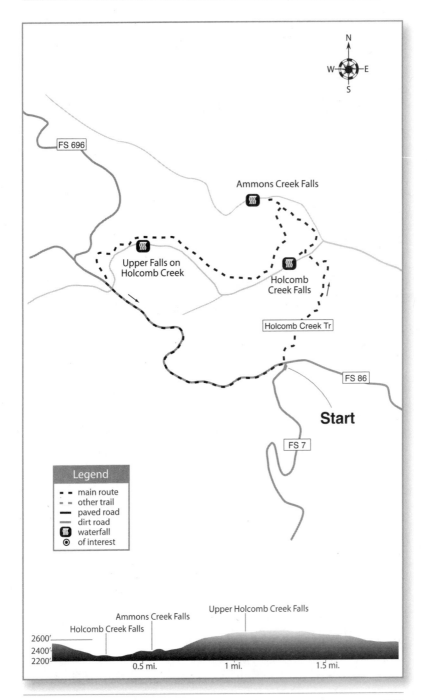

Legend

- - - main route
- - - other trail
—— paved road
—— dirt road
🌊 waterfall
◉ of interest

2600'
2400'
2200'

Holcomb Creek Falls

Ammons Creek Falls

Upper Holcomb Creek Falls

0.5 mi.   1 mi.   1.5 mi.

FS 696

Ammons Creek Falls

Upper Falls on
Holcomb Creek

Holcomb
Creek Falls

Holcomb Creek Tr

FS 86

Start

FS 7

Dicks Creek Falls Trail

Hike Distance:	1.6 miles
Type of Hike:	Loop
Number of Falls:	3
Hiking Time:	1 hour
Dry Feet:	Maybe
Start Elevation:	1,555 ft
Total Ascent:	420 ft
Land Manager:	USFS
Fee:	None

DICKS CREEK FALLS
Class: Horsetail Height: 50 ft Rating: Good

Quiz: In 1968 the U.S. Congress passed the National Wild and Scenic Rivers Act, which President Lyndon Johnson then signed into law. Which river forming the northern border between South Carolina and Georgia was among the first to receive Wild and Scenic status? Answer: The Chattooga River was given the designation in 1974. At the time there were pictures of then Governor Jimmy Carter—a Georgia native, and a huge supporter of the Chattooga who would go on to become President in 1977—in the bow of an aluminum canoe, challenging the river's mighty rapids. How many governors these days do you see doing that?

The Act states: *It is hereby declared to be the policy of the United States that certain selected rivers of the Nation which, with their immediate environments, possess outstandingly remarkable scenic, recreational, geologic, fish and wildlife, historic, cultural, or other similar values, shall be preserved in free-flowing condition, and that they and their immediate environments shall be protected for the benefit and enjoyment of pres-*

ent and future generations. The Congress declares that the established national policy of dam and other construction at appropriate sections of the rivers of the United States needs to be complemented by a policy that would preserve other selected rivers or sections thereof in their free-flowing condition to protect the water quality of such rivers and to fulfill other vital national conservation purposes.

That's a dense paragraph. Essentially what it means is that the Chattooga River will remain undeveloped in perpetuity, along with the corridor of land within a quarter of a mile of its banks.

From the Chattooga's headwaters near Cashiers, NC, all the way to its end at Lake Tugaloo in South Carolina, 39.8 miles of it are classified as "wild," 2.5 miles are classified as "scenic," and 14.6 miles are classified as "recreational."

The section you'll hike to on this route is both wild *and* scenic. Once you arrive at the riverbank and look out over

Dicks Creek Ledge just upstream of Dicks Creek Falls, there will be no question in your mind that the Chattooga deserves every bit of protection the National Wild and Scenic Rivers Act provides. Although in some places it spans a mere 30 feet, here at Dicks Creek Ledge the river is close to 100 yards wide. The entire river plunges over an 8-foot-high broken ledge with giant boulders strewn all around it. Immediately downstream of the ledge, Dicks Creek Falls plummets into the river. Imagine what President Carter must have thought when he rounded the bend in his canoe and this scene came into view. No wonder he urged Congress to preserve it.

DICKS CREEK LEDGE
Class: Rapid Height: 8 ft Rating: Fair

Dicks Creek Falls Trail (cont.)

Getting to the Trailhead

From Clayton, take Warwoman Road for 5.9 miles and turn right on Sandy Ford Road. Go 0.6 mile and bear left as the road turns to gravel. Continue another 3.4 miles and park just before the road fords Dicks Creek.

GPS Coordinates

N 34° 52.23' W 83° 15.19'

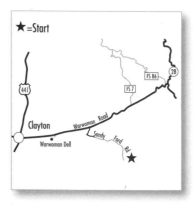

Hiking Directions

Begin Walk downstream on the unmarked but well-worn trail along the left side of Dicks Creek.

Mile 0.5 Cross the Bartram and Chattooga River Trail onto a small footbridge and Dicks Creek Trail.

Mile 0.6 Reach Dicks Creek Slide, a 12-foot waterfall just 100 feet or so above the lip of

Dicks Creek Falls on the right side of the trail. After viewing, continue down to the river on Dicks Creek Falls Trail.

Mile 0.7 Reach the Chattooga River. Dicks Creek Ledge spans the entire 100-yard width of the river here, while just below, Dicks Creek Falls cascades down into it. It's a beautiful spot; some nice big boulders here make a great place for a snack or lunch break. When you're ready, return to the Bartram/Chattooga River Trail intersection.

Mile 0.9 Turn left on Bartram/Chattooga River Trail.

Mile 1.2 Turn right on the Bartram Trail at the fork. The Chattooga River trail exits left.

Mile 1.3 Turn right on Sandy Ford Road.

Mile 1.6 Finish.

DICKS CREEK SLIDE
Class: Waterslide Height: 12 ft Rating: Fair

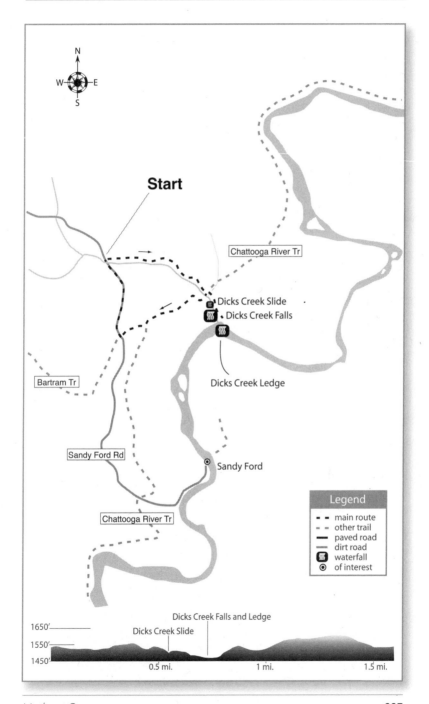

Start

Chattooga River Tr

Dicks Creek Slide
Dicks Creek Falls

Dicks Creek Ledge

Bartram Tr

Sandy Ford Rd

Sandy Ford

Chattooga River Tr

Legend

- - main route
- - other trail
— paved road
— dirt road
🆇 waterfall
◉ of interest

Dicks Creek Falls and Ledge

1650'
Dicks Creek Slide
1550'
1450'
              0.5 mi.   1 mi.   1.5 mi.

Warwoman Dell–Bartram Trail

Hike Distance:	5 miles
Type of Hike:	Out & Back
Number of Falls:	4
Hiking Time:	Half day
Dry Feet:	Yes
Start Elevation:	1,978 ft
Total Ascent:	1,042 ft
Land Manager:	USFS
Fee:	None

MARTINS CREEK FALLS
Class: Tiered Height: 40 ft Rating: Excellent

The roadside sign reads: *William Bartram Trail. Traced 1773-1777. In 1775, William Bartram wrote in "Travels" of the flora and fauna of this area as he gathered specimens to ship to London.* The few words that fit on the sign barely describe the feats achieved by this extraordinary adventurer and scientist.

In 1773 Bartram, a New Englander, began a journey in Charleston, SC, that would lead him through swamps, along rivers, through dense forest, and ultimately into the high country of North Carolina, just shy of the Great Smoky Mountains. At the time, few Europeans had traveled anywhere in the region. His reason for the trip, as the sign states, was to catalog flora and fauna, collect specimens, and send them to London. He traveled mostly on foot and followed routes established by the Native Americans of the region, the Creek and the Cherokee.

If you read through Bartram's *Travels* (it's still in print), you'll realize he did much more than study and take specimens of plants and animals. His book thoroughly describes the entire region, making notes of human

WARWOMAN DELL FALLS
Class: Tiered Height: 20 ft Rating: Fair

36.4 miles are in Georgia. If the trail were to cover the entirety of Bartram's travels as originally planned, it would stretch 2,550 miles through eight states.

On this route you'll get just a small taste of the Bartram Trail as it winds out of Warwoman Dell over to Martins Creek—but what a delightful taste. You'll see four waterfalls along the route and stroll through the very pretty Warwoman Dell. Each of the falls encountered is a treat for the eyes as well as the other senses, and the trail is well marked and easy to follow. If only William Bartram had had it so easy.

interaction and characteristics of the landscape. And for Bartram it was a physically uncomfortable trip. Much of his travel through the area was during the heat of summer. This was a fellow used to cool New England summers, not the hot and humid conditions typical in the South at that time of year. He was most certainly fed upon by biting insects and probably got at least one good case of poison ivy—he was, after all, collecting specimens.

The Bartram Trail follows William Bartram's route from the Foothills Parkway in South Carolina across the Chattooga River into Georgia, to its northern terminus atop North Carolina's Cheoah Bald. Of its 115.4-mile-length,

BECKY BRANCH FALLS
Class: Tiered Height: 30 ft Rating: Good

Warwoman Dell–Bartram Trail (cont.)

Getting to the Trailhead

From Clayton, take Warwoman Road 2.9 miles to Warwoman Dell Recreation Area on the right. Drive to the trailhead parking at the end of the road in the picnic area.

GPS Coordinates
N 34° 52.89′ W 83° 21.17′

Hiking Directions

Begin First do a mini-loop, walking out the back of the parking lot and alongside the small stream on the Warwoman Dell Interpretive Trail.

Mile 0.25 Warwoman Falls, a 20-foot drop on a small stream, is at the head of the loop.

Mile 0.5 Back at the trailhead, walk down the road through the picnic area and bear left onto the yellow diamond–blazed Bartram Trail. You'll go up and across Warwoman Road.

Mile 0.8 Cross on a footbridge just below 30-foot-high Becky Branch Falls. After observing the

falls, continue on the Bartram Trail as it winds around the ridge to the next watershed.

Mile 2.5 Here you'll pass the lower falls on Martins Creek. Down on the right, it's a 12-foot tiered drop followed by a pothole-filled sluice.

Mile 2.7 Reach Martins Creek Falls. There are two observation decks here. The upper deck looks out at the high waterfall, while from the lower deck you look down into a sluice that forms the lower section of the falls. Return the way you came from here.

Mile 5.0 Finish.

Lower Falls on Martins Creek
Class: Tiered Height: 12 ft Rating: Fair

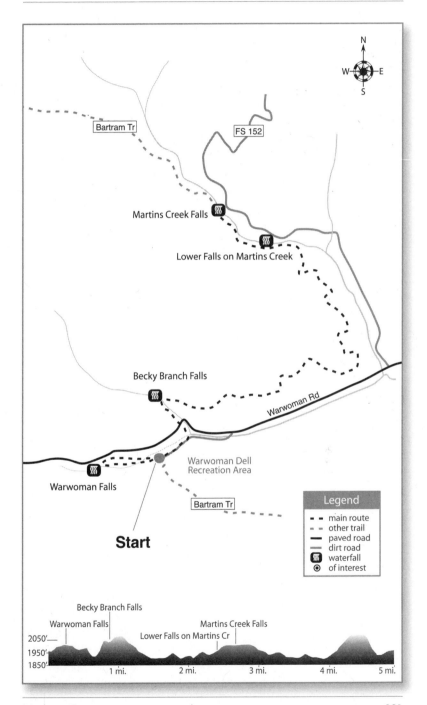

N
W   E
S

Bartram Tr

FS 152

Martins Creek Falls

Lower Falls on Martins Creek

Becky Branch Falls

Warwoman Rd

Warwoman Dell
Recreation Area

Warwoman Falls

Bartram Tr

Start

Legend
- - main route
- - other trail
— paved road
— dirt road
waterfall
of interest

Becky Branch Falls

Warwoman Falls

Martins Creek Falls

Lower Falls on Martins Cr

2050'
1950'
1850'

1 mi.   2 mi.   3 mi.   4 mi.   5 mi.

Bull Sluice

Hike Distance:	1.4 miles
Type of Hike:	Out & Back
Number of Falls:	3
Hiking Time:	2 hours
Dry Feet:	No
Start Elevation:	1,277 ft
Total Ascent:	514 ft
Land Manager:	USFS
Fee:	None

BULL SLUICE RAPID
Class: Rapid Height: 10 ft Rating: Fair

Give yourself plenty of time for this hike, but not because it's long and difficult. On the contrary, it's short and easy. Spring, summer, and fall, on almost any day—and especially on weekends—Bull Sluice is a happening place. At regular intervals whitewater raft trips make their way through the rapid. Stick around long enough, and you're bound to see a rafting party come through. Interspersed between the raft trips are groups of kayakers and canoeists. It's fun to kick back and see how all these folks negotiate the drop. And if it's really hot and sunny, expect to find a few local youths brave enough (or foolish enough) to jump right into the foaming trough and shoot the rapid in nothing but a swimsuit. It all makes for an exciting destination and a fun way to spend a couple of hours.

The great thing about this hike is that it takes you up the Georgia side of the river. This is the side on which river runners get out and scout the rapid from the giant boulder next to the sluice. Most folks walk in from the South Carolina side, where there is a crowded viewing platform. Looking over there at those folks, you gotta know they're wishing they were in your shoes, over on the boulder where the real action is. And since you're here, looking like one of the experts, you might as well know what you're looking at.

Bull Sluice is a Class V rapid on a rating system that goes as high as Class VI. Simply put, it's a difficult and dangerous rapid to negotiate. Difficult because the approach is long and the drops are at odd angles to one another, causing the current to push you one way while you need to be going another; dangerous because of what you can't see. Under the water are numerous potholes in the ledge. Fall out and get your feet caught in one of them, and your body is going to be trapped underwater for hours, if not days.

Watch the raft trips closely as they come through. Almost always they'll send one of the guides down to the base of the rapid to set a safety rope. The guide stands there, ready to throw a rope to anyone who might fall out of the raft during their run. Look at how the boats line up as they come through. They'll space out evenly so each one gets through safely before the next comes along.

At normal water levels the rafts run the double drops through the foamy-looking "top hole" and just to the right of an underwater rock nicknamed "decap." See how the guides position the rafts so that they drop over perpendicular to the top ledge, which is at a right angle to the flow of the river. The crew paddles hard to turn the boat to face the big rock you're standing on. Seconds before they drop over the ledge, listen for the guide to yell, "set!" You'll know he did if the entire crew piles into the bottom of the raft. The guide then expertly turns the boat to face downstream again so it's lined up correctly for the second ledge, which is easy if they get the first one right.

This is how it *should* be done, but you'll see all sorts of runs— rafts get spun around backwards, and people fall out. Sometimes the entire raft flips over and everyone swims. The guide setting the safety rope gets a real workout. And, thank goodness, most all the time, like those youngsters who wash through in their swimsuits, everyone comes through just fine.

Bull Sluice (cont.)

Getting to the Trailhead

From Clayton, take US 76 east for 9.0 miles and cross the Chattooga River into South Carolina. Turn left and park in the lower portion of the river access parking lot.

GPS Coordinates
N 34° 48.88′ W 83° 18.30′

Hiking Directions

Begin Walk out the bottom of the parking lot, down the steps and turn right to cross the bridge back into Georgia.

Mile 0.2 Turn right on the Chattooga River Trail.

Mile 0.3 At the fork, turn right off Chattooga River Trail down to the river. Once alongside the river, walk upstream through the rock jumbles. It's a well-beaten route and easy to follow. You can see Bull Sluice up ahead. Please note: Should the river be in flood you will not be able to go this way, but you can still access Bull Sluice from the South Carolina side.

Mile 0.6 Ford Poke Creek. There are two small slide waterfalls just upstream on this creek. You can check them out now or on the return.

Mile 0.7 Reach the bottom of Bull Sluice Rapid. You can observe the drop and watch any boaters coming through from here or scramble up on the big rock above the rapid for a better view. Hang out here as long as you like, then return the way you came.

Mile 1.4 Finish.

TOP SLIDE FALLS ON POKE CREEK
Class: Waterslide Height: 10 ft Rating: Fair

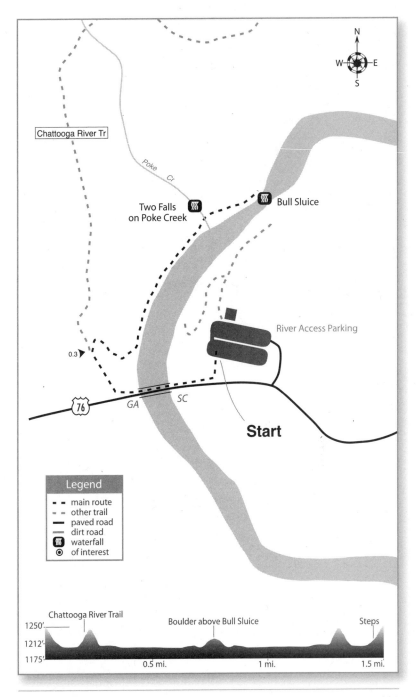

Chattooga River Tr

Poke Cr

Two Falls
on Poke Creek

Bull Sluice

River Access Parking

0.3 ▶

76 GA SC

Start

Legend
- - main route
- - other trail
— paved road
— dirt road
🌊 waterfall
◉ of interest

Chattooga River Trail

Boulder above Bull Sluice

Steps

1250'
1212'
1175'

0.5 mi.   1 mi.   1.5 mi.

Darnell Creek Falls

Hike Distance:	0.5 mile
Type of Hike:	Out & Back
Number of Falls:	1
Hiking Time:	30 min
Dry Feet:	Yes
Start Elevation:	2,292 ft
Total Ascent:	25 ft
Land Manager:	USFS
Fee:	None

DARNELL CREEK FALLS
Class: Sluice Height: 20 ft Rating: Fair

Darnell Creek Falls is a very pretty little waterfall that's easy to get to and not far off the main road at Rabun Gap, north of Clayton. Right across the road is Rabun Gap–Nacoochee School, a private boarding school and home of the *Foxfire* books. On a warm spring or fall day, you may run into students from the school swimming in the plunge pool below the falls. The walk is more of a leg-stretcher than a hike. In fact, you can drive on the old woods road almost up to the base if you have a vehicle with good clearance. It's not a waterfall you should go out of your way for, but if you're nearby, you may want to check it out.

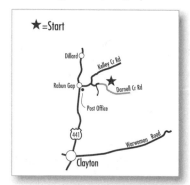

★=Start

Dillard

Kelley Cr Rd

Rabun Gap

Darnell Cr Rd

Post Office

441

Warwoman Road

Clayton

Getting to the Trailhead

From Clayton, drive north on US 441 to the Rabun Gap Post Office. Turn right onto Kellys Creek Road. Go 1.0 mile and turn right on Darnell Creek Road. Continue 0.4 mile and bear left at the fork with the private Chestnut Mountain Road. Drive down across the bridge and bear right for another 0.3 mile. Park at the fork in the road.

GPS Coordinates

N 34° 57.53' W 83° 21.38'

Hiking Directions

Begin From the fork, take the right fork on the old wood road.

Mile 0.25 Darnell Creek Falls. After viewing, return the way you came.

Mile 0.5 Finish.

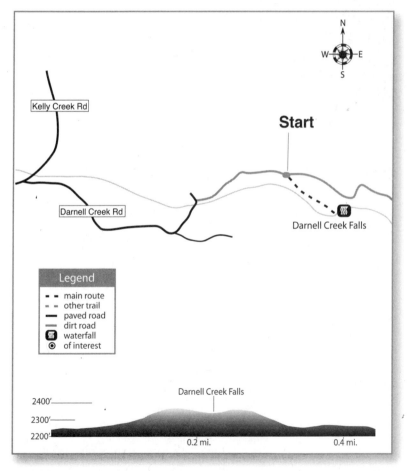

Tate City

Hike Distance:	1 mile
Type of Hike:	Out & Back
Number of Falls:	2
Hiking Time:	1 hour
Dry Feet:	No
Start Elevation:	2,249 ft
Total Ascent:	300 ft
Land Manager:	USFS
Fee:	None

DENTON BRANCH FALLS
Class: Horsetail Height: 30 ft Rating: Good

Tate City is anything but a city—it's not even close. It was originally a mining community, then a logging camp. The founders must have had big plans when they named it. Drive there today, and you'll find one of the remotest communities in north Georgia. If Tallulah River Road washed out in a flood, those folks would be stranded. They probably wouldn't mind.

Once in Tate City, you'll find a shopping mall, a community center, and a few houses. A shopping mall? Just kidding. Look for a ragged old log building with a sign on the side reading "Tate City Mall," just off the road. It might be described as an open air mall, since the chinking between the logs is long gone; isolation tends to add a little quirkiness to peoples' sense of humor. But it's no wonder folks still live here—the location is idyllic. Mountains surround a relatively wide valley, with room enough for farm fields. The upper Tallulah River runs right down the middle of it. Best of all, there's a beautiful waterfall just out of "town" on Denton Branch, and another you can walk to whenever you head down the road to do some shopping—that is, if they're out of everything at the Tate City Mall.

The hike up to Denton Branch Falls is a pleasant one, and nearly anyone who doesn't mind getting their feet wet can do it. Once you locate the road to the trailhead, drive up to the first pullout and park on the right.

The hike starts out as a continuation of the old road. After you ford the creek you'll be on an unmarked but well-used footpath. Follow it on up the stream, and enjoy the noise Denton Branch makes just off to your right. Soon you'll come to the lower waterfall on Denton Branch. This water-slide/sluice drops 30 feet, spread out over a horizontal distance of 30 feet.

Continue up from here just a short distance to the main attraction, Denton Branch Falls. This pretty waterfall forms a horsetail as it cascades 30 feet, crashes into a pile of boulders, then rushes on down the mountain.

This is a nice hike, but perhaps too short, given the distance you've driven to get here. To make up for that, be sure to take advantage of the proximity of Flat Branch Falls on your return.

Bonus Falls

FLAT BRANCH FALLS
Class: Tiered Height: 150 feet
Rating: Excellent

You'll pass the trailhead for this short but steep hike—a real huffer-puffer—to Flat Branch Falls on your way to Tate City. Watch your odometer closely to find it. From the intersection of Persimmon Road and Tallulah River Road, drive 3.3 miles and park just beyond the bridge over the Tallulah River. Or, from the trailhead for Denton Branch Falls, drive 3.3 miles and park just before crossing the bridge. From there, cross the bridge on foot, take an immediate left, and scramble up the unmarked but well-used trail. The first 20 feet are pretty steep. The trail leads up to the base of the falls—a very high, tiered horsetail falling over a cliff face. In all, you'll hike about 0.4 mile. The trailhead coordinates are below.

GPS: N 34° 56.78' W 83° 33.02'

Tate City (cont.)

Getting to the Trailhead

From Clayton, take US 76 west for 8.0 miles and turn right on Persimmon Road. Drive 4.2 miles and turn left on Tallulah River Road. Continue another 6.5 miles to the bridge over Denton Branch. Just before the bridge, turn onto the unmarked road and drive 0.1 mile. Park at the first pullout.

GPS Coordinates

N 34° 59.04' W 83° 33.18'

Hiking Directions

Begin Walk up the roadbed, ford the creek, and continue up and around the dirt mound to walk alongside the creek. The trail is not marked, but is well used.

Mile 0.2 At the trail fork, go right to continue hiking alongside the creek.

Mile 0.3 Reach lower falls on Denton Branch, a 30-foot waterslide. Continue along the creek.

Mile 0.5 Reach the base of Denton Branch Falls, a 30-foot

horsetail falling into a jumble of boulders. When you've had enough viewing, return the way you hiked in.

Mile 1.0 Finish.

LOWER FALLS ON DENTON BRANCH
Class: Waterslide Height: 30 ft Rating: Fair

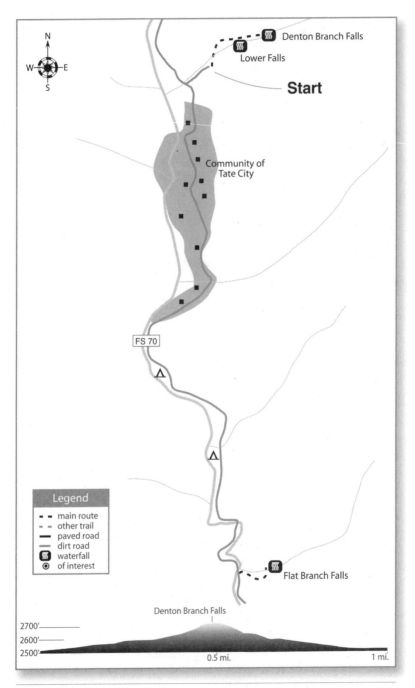

Denton Branch Falls

Lower Falls

Start

Community of
Tate City

FS 70

Legend

- - main route
- - other trail
— paved road
— dirt road
waterfall
of interest

Flat Branch Falls

Denton Branch Falls

2700'
2600'
2500'

0.5 mi.   1 mi.

Hemlock Falls Trail

Hike Distance:	3.4 miles
Type of Hike:	Out & Back
Number of Falls:	6
Hiking Time:	Half day
Dry Feet:	No
Start Elevation:	2,025 ft
Total Ascent:	615 ft
Land Manager:	USFS
Fee:	None

HEMLOCK FALLS
Class: Fan Height: 15 ft Rating: Good

Hemlock Falls is one of at least five waterfalls located on Moccasin Creek, a stream that feeds into Lake Burton at Moccasin Creek State Park. Driving to the trailhead along GA 197, you'll pass what seems like a beehive of activity. This twisty, curvy road is the main access to many vacation homes on the lake. It leaves the highway at the entrance to the state park and the Georgia State Fish Hatchery. People seem to be everywhere—carrying fishing poles, pulling campers, eating picnics. On the short drive to the trail, you'll leave all this behind and enter quiet woods. It's a nice feeling.

Once on the trail, you don't have to hike too far before you begin spotting waterfalls. If you're observant and the weather hasn't been too dry, the first falls you'll see is across the creek and just up in the woods. It's formed by a small tributary feeding into Moccasin Creek. Two more falls on Moccasin Creek itself soon follow. Both are down off the trail, so to get a good view you'll need to scramble down the short goatpaths made by hikers who came before you. Look for one falls 8 feet high and one 10 feet high.

Farther along you'll cross a very narrow bridge that might seem a bit dicey. Just hold your breath and try not to think about the small waterfall below. Just above the bridge, begin looking down to the left for the third waterfall, a 12-foot block falls followed immediately by a 10-foot waterslide spread out over 30 horizontal feet. And there are still two waterfalls yet to see!

Hemlock Falls is next. You'll find it at a large flat area, dropping 15 feet into a big plunge

FIRST FALLS ON MOCCASIN CREEK
Class: Sluice Height: 8 ft Rating: Fair

pool. If you need to cool off, this is the place to do it. It's also a good place for a break before starting the next leg of the hike.

When you leave Hemlock Falls you'll notice the trail is not as well worn or maintained. This is because most hikers turn around at this point. They're on Hemlock Falls Trail, and they've reached Hemlock Falls, so they don't see a reason to continue. But there's a very good reason to: The uppermost falls on Moccasin Creek is the cream of the waterfalls on this hike, and you've got just 0.6 mile to go.

Above Hemlock Falls, pay close attention to the hike directions. You want to be sure you get over to the other side of the creek above the falls. It's tricky because it looks like the trail continues up the same side of the stream you're

TRIBUTARY FEEDER FALLS
Class: Plunge Height: 15 ft Rating: Nice

THIRD FALLS ON MOCCASIN CREEK
Class: Block/Sluice Height: 22 ft Rating: Good

the pool, then head on back to the trailhead. While you're walking along, think about this.

Hemlock Falls got its name from the Eastern hemlock, an evergreen that thrives in the riparian zones (land adjacent to streams and rivers) of our Southern Appalachians. You'll see hemlock trees on most every waterfall hike you take. Now imagine this: What would these zones look like with no hemlock trees? Well, they would look vastly different. The dark, cooling shade the trees produce is an essential element. Without them, streams that hold trout would

on. Don't follow that false trail; it ends in a tangle of rhododendron. Cross over the creek as the directions say, and follow the trail as it heads high above the creek.

Before you know it, you'll be at your final destination, the fifth and highest waterfall on Moccasin Creek. Facing it from the large plunge pool at the bottom, you'll see three tiers cascading down the left side of its pourover cliff, while a horsetail falls down over the far right side. It's as if the creek is pouring over the rim of a bowl—a bowl in which you are standing. Enjoy the view, or if it's warm enough, cool off with a dip in

FIFTH FALLS ON MOCCASIN CREEK
Class: Tiered/Horsetail Height: 40 ft Rating: Excellent

likely warm up and the fish would not survive. Deep-shade-loving plants, like rhododendron, would suffer. Humans would get hotter and sweatier while hiking. The whole ecology would be altered if the hemlocks were gone.

Unfortunately, this scenario might well come to pass. Our Eastern hemlocks are under attack by an exotic pest known as the hemlock woolly adelgid. This tiny aphid-like bug literally sucks the life out of the tree. Once an infestation begins, the tree will survive only about four years. Drive north through North Carolina and into Virginia, and you'll see whole mountainsides of dead hemlocks. It's a sad sight.

Research scientists are racing against the clock to find a way to save these trees. But it's a complex problem. Spraying insecticide works, but how do you spray millions of trees? Finding and introducing a natural predator may work, but can it be done in time? The best hopes lie with nature herself and the trees that survive. The hope is that the hemlock itself will evolve to withstand the threat.

Bonus Falls

UPPER FALLS ON WILDCAT CREEK
Class: Tiered Height: 25 ft
Rating: Good

These two waterfalls are very near the Hemlock Falls trailhead. To get there, continue on GA 197 past the fish hatchery for 1.3 miles. Turn right on Wildcat Road and go 1.4 miles. The falls are just off the left side of the road.

LOWER FALLS ON WILDCAT CREEK
Class: Tiered Height: 30 ft
Rating: Good

Hemlock Falls Trail (cont.)

Getting to the Trailhead

From Clayton, take US 76 west for 11.0 miles and turn left on GA 197. Go 3.7 miles to Moccasin Creek State Park and the state fish hatchery. Turn right at the sign for Hemlock Falls. It's 0.5 mile to the trailhead.

GPS Coordinates
N 34° 50.87' W 83° 35.82'

Persimmon Rd
441
197
76
Clayton
Lake Burton
Moccasin Creek
State Park
Bonus Falls
Wildcat Creek Rd
★=Start

Hiking Directions

Begin Walk out beyond the stone trail sign and up alongside Moccasin Creek.

Mile 0.4 Pass a small feeder stream falls which you can see on the far side of Moccasin Creek.

Mile 0.5 Reach the first falls on Moccasin Creek, an 8-foot-high sluice. Continue on the trail.

Mile 0.6 Reach the second falls on Moccasin Creek, a 10-foot-high sluice. Continue on the trail.

Mile 0.7 Cross the creek on a narrow footbridge right over the top of a small waterfall.

Mile 0.8 Reach the third falls on Moccasin Creek, a 12-foot-high drop followed by a 10-foot-high, 30-foot-long slide. Continue on the trail.

Mile 1.1 Reach Hemlock Falls, a 15-foot horsetail fan landing in a magnificent pool. Continue on up the right side of the falls. Up to this point you've been following a well-defined trail. As you ascend beyond Hemlock Falls, the trail becomes fainter and less well maintained. **Pay close attention here.** From the top of Hemlock Falls, step off 60 or so paces, then ford to the other side of Moccasin Creek, where the trail continues as you climb high above the creek.

Mile 1.7 Reach the fifth and uppermost falls on Moccasin Creek, the sixth waterfall of the hike. This is the best of the bunch, with a 40-foot triple tier on the left and a horsetail on the right, both landing in a nice pool. When you're ready, return the way you came.

Mile 3.4 Finish.

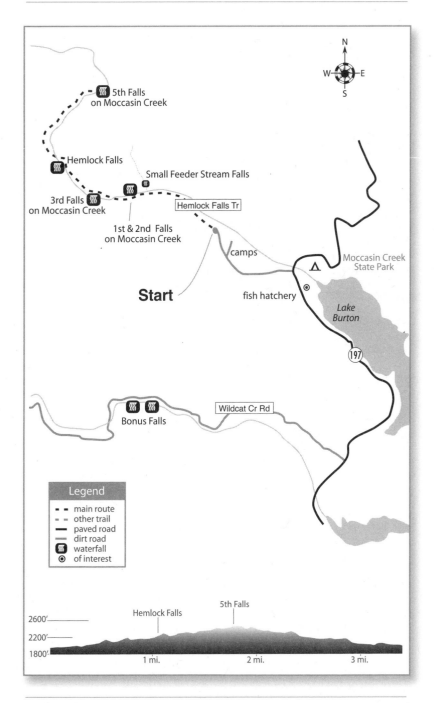

N

W   E

S

5th Falls
on Moccasin Creek

Hemlock Falls

Small Feeder Stream Falls

3rd Falls
on Moccasin Creek

Hemlock Falls Tr

1st & 2nd Falls
on Moccasin Creek

camps

Start

Moccasin Creek
State Park

fish hatchery

*Lake
Burton*

197

Bonus Falls

Wildcat Cr Rd

Legend
- - main route
- - other trail
— paved road
— dirt road
☶ waterfall
◉ of interest

2600'
2200'
1800'

Hemlock Falls

5th Falls

1 mi.   2 mi.   3 mi.

Stonewall Falls

Hike Distance:	1.7 miles
Type of Hike:	T-Shape
Number of Falls:	3
Hiking Time:	1 hour
Dry Feet:	Yes
Start Elevation:	1,990 ft
Total Ascent:	310 ft
Land Manager:	USFS
Fee:	None

STONEWALL FALLS
Class: Horsetail Height: 20 ft Rating: Good

It's possible to drive all the way to the base of Stonewall Falls, and you could do that and call it good. After all, the road does end there. But why would you want to drive when you can get in a short hike—and see two additional waterfalls in the bargain?

The parking lot for this hike is at the trailhead for two mountain bike routes, one called Stonewall Falls Loop and the other known as White Twister. Many of the trails in north Georgia are meant for foot travel only, but these two are shared with mountain bikers. Back in the early 1990s these cyclists, with their flashy fat-tire bicycles, were the new kids on the block. They flocked to the mountains by the thousands—mostly in groups of three or four—looking for places to ride off-road. Back then their choices were limited to a few trails and a lot more forest roads. This was not good. The available trails quickly became overused, and more than one cyclist strayed onto the footpaths. So the mountain bikers got organized. Clubs were formed, and before you knew it, bikers showed up in the woods in work boots and jeans, and with the help of the Forest Service, began building trails for mountain biking. White Twister Trail and Stonewall Falls Loop Trail are good examples of their efforts. By linking abandoned forest roads and logging rail grades with sections of new trail, they created some nice routes.

On this hike you'll walk only a short distance on the White Twister Trail, but there's a good chance you'll run into a mountain biker or two. Most of these folks follow the International Mountain Biking Association "Rules of the Trail," so follow their lead as to what to do should you meet. If they stick to the guidelines, they'll yield the trail to you. Don't be

FIRST FALLS ON STONEWALL CREEK
Class: Tiered Height: 15 ft Rating: Fair

SECOND FALLS ON STONEWALL CREEK
Class: Slide/Tier Height: 12 ft Rating: Fair

surprised if they hop off their bikes and strike up a conversation; that's the idea. All users are friends (not foes), and talking helps everyone to get along.

While Stonewall Falls is directly adjacent to the road, the other two waterfalls take a little bit more effort to see. It's a steep but short pitch to get down to them and equally steep coming back up. You'll have to scramble on each one. Once down at the creek, you'll find they were well worth the effort.

Stonewall Falls (cont.)

Getting to the Trailhead

From Tiger on Old US 441 south of Clayton, drive 2.4 miles and turn right on FS 20. Continue another 1.3 bumpy miles to the trailhead parking lot on the right for Stonewall Falls and White Twister Trails.

GPS Coordinates
N 34° 49.46′ W 83° 26.68′

Hiking Directions

Begin Walk out of the parking lot and back down to FS 20, then turn right.

Mile 0.2 Turn left off the road, walk downhill, and turn left again onto White Twister Trail.

Mile 0.6 The first waterfall is on your right. You can hear it from the trail, but you may not see it. Follow the sound. It's a short scramble down the steep hill to the falls, a 15-foot, multi-tiered drop. Scramble back up to the trail and continue downstream.

Mile 0.7 The second waterfall is, again, way down off the trail to your right. Same as before, follow your ears and scramble down to see it. Once back on the trail, head back the way you came past the first falls and go all the way to FS 20.

Mile 0.9 Turn left on FS 20 and walk down the road.

Mile 1.1 Reach Stonewall Falls. The road ends here. Once you've had a good look, return to the trailhead via FS 20.

Mile 1.7 Finish.

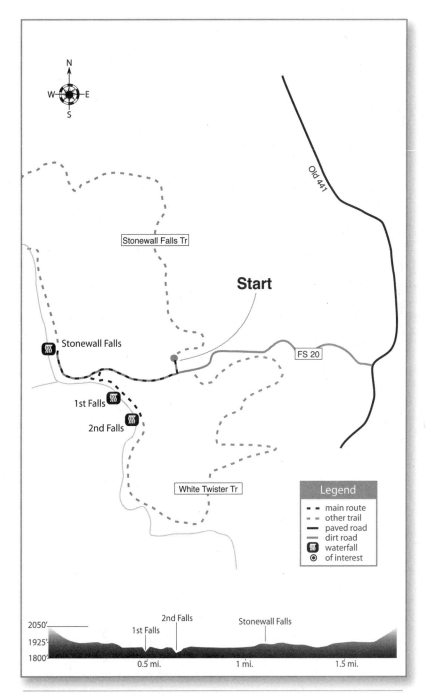

Start

N
W — E
S

Stonewall Falls Tr

Old 441

Stonewall Falls

FS 20

1st Falls

2nd Falls

White Twister Tr

Legend

- - - main route
- - - other trail
—— paved road
—— dirt road
🌊 waterfall
◉ of interest

2050′
1925′
1800′

2nd Falls
1st Falls
Stonewall Falls

0.5 mi.   1 mi.   1.5 mi.

Angel Falls Trail

Hike Distance:	2 miles
Type of Hike:	Out & Back
Number of Falls:	4
Hiking Time:	2 hours
Dry Feet:	Yes
Start Elevation:	1,865 ft
Total Ascent:	538 ft
Land Manager:	USFS
Fee:	$3

ANGEL FALLS
Class: Tiered Height: 80 ft Rating: Excellent

Angel Falls Trail begins and ends at the very pretty Rabun Beach Campground, just across the road from Lake Rabun. This is one of those hikes that most anyone can do without too much trouble. It's a mile up to Angel Falls and a mile back. In the two miles of hiking, you'll pass three additional waterfalls. Something about the way the mountains are put together here gives all these waterfalls a distinctive characteristic and you can see it right away, even in the photos. All of them cascade over thousands of mini-stairsteps. It's as if someone built these mountains by stacking layer after thin layer of rock, one on top of the other. In a sense, that's just what happened. If you were on a college field trip here, your geology professor would describe these falls this way: "The water cascades over a series of nearly horizontal, offset schistose planes in metamorphic rock terrain."

Rabun Beach Campground, like many of the campgrounds managed by the Forest Service, sits on the site of an old Civilian Conservation Corps (CCC) camp. Two hundred men once lived and worked at

PANTHER FALLS
Class: Tiered Height: 50 ft Rating: Good

this particular site, called Camp Rabun. You can read about it and view old photos on the information board at the trailhead. The CCC was formed in the early 1930s for the express purpose of putting people back to work during the Great Depression and jump-starting the economy. All across the country, men lived in camps in the woods and worked at building bridges, roads, and, most important for hikers, foot trails into the wilderness. Many of the trails we use today in north Georgia were built by the "boys of the CCC," as they were affectionately known. They built this trail to Angel Falls. On the hike, look for the remnants of an

old springbox they constructed to collect their drinking water and make a cool place to keep their perishable food.

Hiking up to the various falls is fairly straightforward. There are footbridges across the creek (no need to get your feet wet here) and a viewing platform with a bench at Angel Falls to enhance the view. It's a great place to sit in quiet reflection while the waterfall cascades down in front of you.

Just on the other side of Lake Rabun and a short drive away is Minnehaha Falls (p. 256). The hike to Minnehaha is even shorter, so consider taking in that one as well, on the same day.

FIRST FALLS ON JOE CREEK
Class: Tiered Height: 20 ft Rating: Fair

Angel Falls Trail (cont.)

Getting to the Trailhead

From the entrance to Tallulah Gorge State Park, drive north on US 441 for 1.2 miles and turn left on Old 441. Drive 2.7 miles and turn left on Lake Rabun Road. Continue another 4.7 miles and turn right into Rabun Beach Campground #2. Go another 0.2 mile to the back of the campground and the trailhead.

GPS Coordinates
N 34° 45.65' W 83° 28.35'

Hiking Directions

Begin Walk onto the trail and over the footbridge. Very soon you'll reach the first waterfall on Joe Creek, a 20-foot stairstep falls. Continue on up the trail from here.

Mile 0.3 Pass the springbox mentioned on the information sign at the trailhead.

Mile 0.6 Reach Panther Falls, a 60-foot, near-vertical stairstep

drop. Once you've had a good view, continue on up the trail.

Mile 0.8 Pass another 15-foot stairstep falls, and continue on the trail.

Mile 0.9 The trail forks here. Take either fork to Angel Falls.

Mile 1.0 Reach Angel Falls. A viewing platform with a bench makes a nice place to sit and look at the falls, an 80-foot vertical stairstep drop. The vegetation is so lush it presses in from the sides as if it plans to cover the waterfall. When you're ready, return the way you came.

Mile 2.0 Finish.

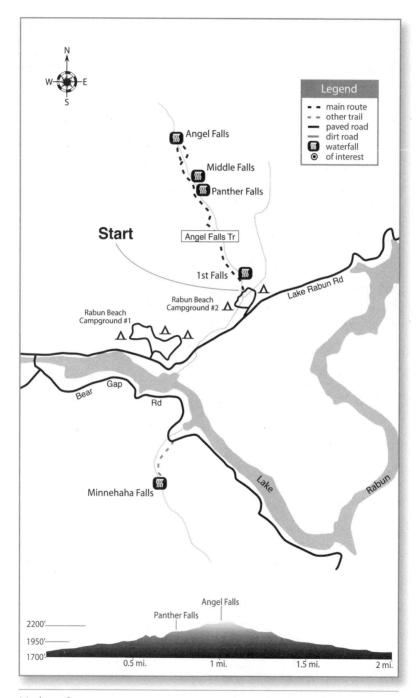

Start

Angel Falls

Middle Falls

Panther Falls

Angel Falls Tr

1st Falls

Rabun Beach
Campground #2

Lake Rabun Rd

Rabun Beach
Campground #1

Bear Gap

Rd

Minnehaha Falls

Lake

Rabun

Legend
main route
other trail
paved road
dirt road
waterfall
of interest

Angel Falls

Panther Falls

2200'
1950'
1700'

0.5 mi.   1 mi.   1.5 mi.   2 mi.

Minnehaha Falls Trail

Hike Distance:	0.5 mile
Type of Hike:	Out & Back
Number of Falls:	1
Hiking Time:	45 min
Dry Feet:	Yes
Start Elevation:	1,740 ft
Total Ascent:	150 ft
Land Manager:	USFS
Fee:	None

MINNEHAHA FALLS
Class: Tiered Height: 75 ft Rating: Excellent

The hike up to Minnehaha Falls is short and sweet. All along the way you'll enjoy the crashing sounds of Falls Creek. It works well to do this hike in conjunction with the hike to Angel Falls, just across the lake (p. 252).

Getting to the Trailhead

From the entrance to Tallulah Gorge State Park, drive north on US 441 for 1.2 miles and turn left on Old 441. Continue 2.7 miles and turn left on Lake Rabun Road. Continue another 6.4 miles and turn left below Seed Dam on Low Gap Road, then turn left again on Bear Gap Road. Drive another 1.5 miles and park at the small pullout on the left, across from trail.

WATERFALL HIKES OF NORTH GEORGIA

GPS Coordinates
N 34° 44.98' W 83° 28.75'

Hiking Directions

Begin Walk across the road and up the rooty trail.

Mile 0.25 Reach Minnehaha Falls. It drops 60 feet to where you are, and then another 15 feet for a total of 75 feet. Return on the trail the way you came.

Mile 0.5 Finish.

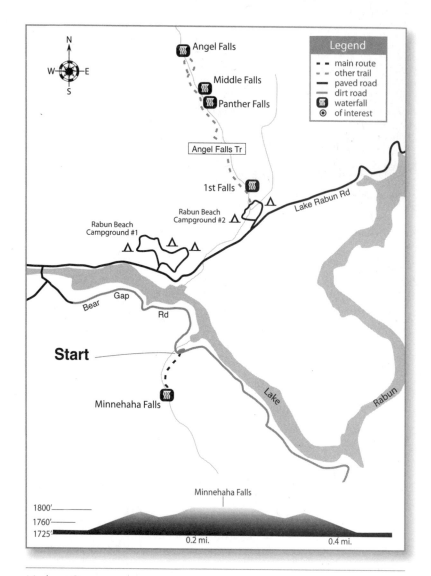

Bad Branch Falls

Hike Distance:	0.4 mile
Type of Hike:	Out & Back
Number of Falls:	1
Hiking Time:	30 min
Dry Feet:	Yes
Start Elevation:	1,911 ft
Total Ascent:	98 ft
Land Manager:	USFS
Fee:	None

BAD BRANCH FALLS
Class: Tiered Height: 30 ft Rating: Good

One of two short hikes along Crow Creek Road, the walk to Bad Branch Falls is nice and easy. Bad Branch crashes over the side of an old quarry to create this waterfall. It's been so long since the quarry was in operation, it's hard to tell that's what it is. Combine this with the hike to Crow Creek (p. 260) for a half-day's outing.

Getting to the Trailhead

From the entrance to Tallulah Gorge State Park, drive north on US 441 for 1.2 miles and turn left on Old 441. Continue 2.7 miles and turn left on Lake Rabun Road. Drive another 6.4 miles and turn left below Seed Dam on Low Gap Road, then turn right on Flat Creek Road. Go another 0.4 mile, turn right on Crow Creek Road, and drive for 2.8 miles. Park in the tiny pullout just before the curve.

GPS Coordinates
N 34° 46.03' W 83° 31.11'

Hiking Directions

Begin Walk onto the trail, which is unsigned but marked by two yellow Georgia Power witness posts. It's wide and well used.

Mile 0.2 Reach Bad Branch Falls, a 30-foot tiered horsetail. From here, return to the start.

Mile 0.4 Finish.

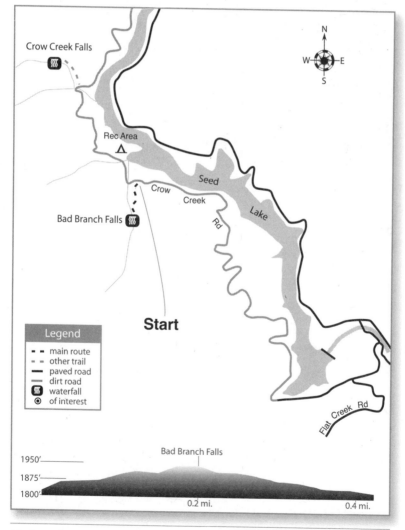

Crow Creek Falls

Hike Distance:	0.4 mile
Type of Hike:	Out & Back
Number of Falls:	1
Hiking Time:	30 min
Dry Feet:	Yes
Start Elevation:	1,797 ft
Total Ascent:	64 ft
Land Manager:	USFS
Fee:	None

CROW CREEK FALLS
Class: Tiered Height: 15 ft Rating: Fair

This is the other short hike along Crow Creek Road. Here you'll walk up to Crow Creek Falls on an old woods trail. Two creeks come together at the start here; be sure to take the one to your right. For a longer excursion, combine this hike with Bad Branch Falls (p. 258).

Getting to the Trailhead

From the entrance to Tallulah Gorge State Park, drive north on US 441 for 1.2 miles and turn left on Old 441. Go 2.7 miles and turn left on Lake Rabun Road. Continue another 6.4 miles and turn left below Seed Dam on Low Gap Road, then right on Flat Creek Road. Drive another 0.4 mile and turn right on Crow Creek Road for 3.6 miles.

WATERFALL HIKES OF NORTH GEORGIA

Park in the tiny pullout in the widest point of the curve.

GPS Coordinates
N 34° 46.44' W 83° 31.48'

Hiking Directions

Begin Walk over the dirt mound and onto the unmarked but well-used trail just to the right of the creek.

Mile 0.2 Reach Crow Creek Falls, a 15-foot tiered plunge. Return from here the way you came.

Mile 0.4 Finish.

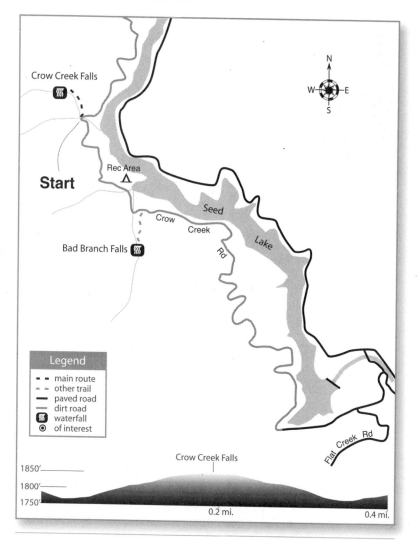

Tallulah Gorge Scramble

Hike Distance:	3.6 miles
Type of Hike:	Loop
Number of Falls:	8
Hiking Time:	Half day
Dry Feet:	No
Start Elevation:	1,556 ft
Total Ascent:	1,002 ft
Land Manager:	State Park
Fee:	$5

HURRICANE FALLS
Class: Horsetail Height: 96 ft Rating: Spectacular

Driving along US 441 south of Clayton and crossing over the dam that forms Tallulah Falls Lake, you'd never guess that Georgia's most rugged gorge is just below. But walk up to the rim and peer down over the cliff at the raging river, and there will be no doubt. In fact, Tallulah Gorge is home to five major waterfalls dropping hundreds of feet over a two-mile stretch. Cliffs walls stand on either shore as tributaries cascade into the river below. One of the tributaries forms Caledonia Cascade, at 600 feet the fifth-highest waterfall east of the Mississippi.

This route is not for the casual hiker. Casual hikers and adventurers should stick to the trails along the rim. Only more agile, fit hikers should tackle the climb down into the gorge, across the footbridge, and then back up the other side. Walking down 500-plus steps on one side and up 500-plus steps on the other gets your heart beating, but it's not a technical challenge. Not only will you see the gorge from the rim and go down and then up all those steps, you'll hike and scramble right down on the floor of the gorge. That's the best way to see the bottom

L'EAU D'OR FALLS
Class: Tiered Height: 46 ft Rating: Excellent

Once on the floor of the gorge, your first obstacle will be crossing to the other side of the river. This requires either near superhuman leaping ability (rock to rock) or wading through waist deep water. Either way, chances are, by the time you get to the other side you'll be wet. Just upstream of the crossing is the 96-foot Hurricane Falls. You crossed over the top of that one on the footbridge, but from down here it seems—*and is*—huge.

Now the real fun begins. Basically, all you have to do is three of the five big waterfalls and become more a participant than a spectator.

Hiking the gorge floor requires a permit. Permits are issued to the first 100 or so folks each day, so to get one, you'll want to show up early at the interpretive center. For safety reasons, permits are not issued during inclement weather, so pick a nice day. Besides getting there early for the permit, it's a good idea to start in the morning, since you won't want to rush. The permit carries no charge in addition to the entry fee, but everyone gets a talk from the ranger about safety precautions and what to expect.

TEMPESTA FALLS
Class: Fan Height: 76 ft Rating: Spectacular

OCEANA FALLS
Class: Waterslide Height: 50 ft Rating: Spectacular

keep your feet from slipping on the rock. Just below Caledonia and alongside Oceana and Bridal Veil you'll need to traverse a stretch of steeply angled rock. The "grippier" your shoes, the better (leave the stiff boots at home today), since a slip could mean scraped flesh and possibly a dunking in the water below. Pick your route carefully. In the case of Oceana and Bridal Veil, stay well left of the falls, lower your center of gravity by getting on all fours,

work your way down the left side of the gorge. There is no marked trail, but you can see where folks have been before. Much of the time you'll be climbing over, around, and between river boulders. By the time it's all over, you'll also get pretty good at hopping from one to the next. It's really not too difficult; just don't expect to move quickly.

The real challenges come in the areas around Oceana and Bridal Veil Falls, as well as at the base of Caledonia Cascade. At these locations, the more rock-climbing experience you've had, the more comfortable you're likely to be. The kind of hiking you'll be doing will resemble what are known in the climbing world as friction moves. In other words, you are relying on friction to

BOTTOM TIER OF CALEDONIA CASCADE
Class: Tiered Height: 600 ft Rating: Fair

and stay off anything that is wet or looks wet. Don't be embarrassed to scoot along on your rear if necessary. It's an exciting place to be, with a roaring waterslide just over your right shoulder.

Park rules allow you to go down as far as the bottom of Bridal Veil Falls. There's a plunge pool here the size of a small lake, and it's a great place to swim or have picnic or both. From this pool you should be able to spot two more waterfalls cascading from the cliffs above. One is just downstream on the left, the other much farther downstream on the right. Look high up on the cliff to see it. Hang out here as long as you like, but remember, you have to get back to the footbridge over the same terrain you covered on the way down.

Aside from the gorge floor, the remainder of the hike takes in all the overlooks that let you peer into the gorge from high above. It's fun to look down on the waterfalls and pick out where you were earlier in the day.

Be sure also to plan a visit to the interpretive center. It has

BRIDAL VEIL FALLS
Class: Waterslide Height: 17 ft Rating: Good

interesting displays ranging from how the gorge was formed to the local plants and wildlife to past adventurers, including actors and stunt men who were in the film *Deliverance* (see p. 138).

TRIBUTARY FALLS BELOW BRIDAL VEIL ON LEFT
Class: Tiered Height: 500 ft Rating: Fair

Tallulah Gorge Scramble (cont.)

Getting to the Trailhead

Jane Hurt Yarn Interpretive Center at Tallulah Gorge State Park, just off US 441, south of Clayton.

GPS Coordinates

N 34° 44.41' W 83° 23.42'

Hiking Directions

Begin From the interpretive center, go left on North Rim Trail. Remember your permit!

Mile 0.2 Reach overlook #1. Here you'll see the remains of the Wallenda Tower and look down on Oceana Falls. Return the way you came, passing the interpretive center.

Mile 0.5 Reach overlook #3. View Hawthorne Pool. Turn left onto Hurricane Falls Trail.

Mile 0.5 Reach overlook #2. View Tempesta Falls. The steps to the bottom start here. You'll descend them and cross the footbridge above Hurricane Falls, then turn left down the steps to the gorge floor.

Mile 0.7 Reach the gorge floor and Hurricane Falls viewing platform. Ford the river here and turn right to rock-scramble downstream.

Mile 1.0 Reach Oceana Falls area. Cross underneath Caledonia Cascade, then work your way down the slab far to the left of Oceana, using friction to keep you on the rock.

Mile 1.4 Reach Bridal Veil Falls. There is a large pool here where swimming is allowed. It's a good thing, since you might get wet anyway if you slip while working your way down the rock by the falls. A tributary waterfall falls into the gorge on the left just below the pool, and if you look far down the gorge to the right, you'll see another tributary falls high up on the cliff. Return to the footbridge the way you came.

TRIBUTARY FALLS FAR BELOW BRIDAL VEIL
Class: Tiered Height: 600 ft Rating: Fair

Mile 2.2 Back at Hurricane Falls, cross the river and climb steps up to the south rim.

Mile 2.5 Reach the top steps. Whew! Turn left to overlook #8.

Mile 2.6 Reach overlook #9 and then overlook #10. Retrace your steps to Hurricane Falls Trail, then continue straight on the South Rim Trail.

Mile 2.8- Reach overlook #7.

Mile 2.9 Reach overlook #6.

Mile 3.0 Cross bridge and turn right on North Rim Trail.

Mile 3.2 Reach overlook #5.

Mile 2.3 Reach overlook #4.

Mile 3.5 Reach overlook #3. Return from here to the interpretive center.

Mile 3.6 Finish.

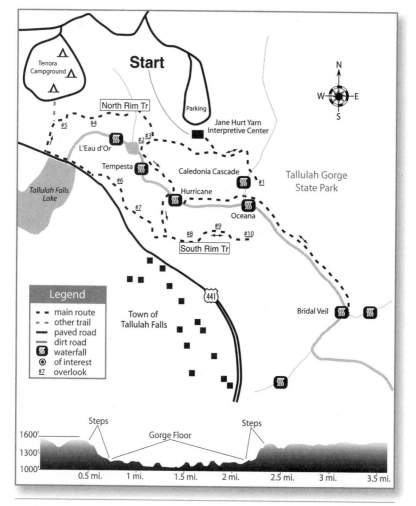

Panther Creek Trail

Hike Distance:	7.8 miles
Type of Hike:	Out & Back
Number of Falls:	4
Hiking Time:	Full day
Dry Feet:	Yes
Start Elevation:	1,509 ft
Total Ascent:	1,147 ft
Land Manager:	USFS
Fee:	$3

PANTHER CREEK FALLS
Class: Tiered   Height: 75 ft   Rating: Spectacular

Fearful of heights? If you are, you might not enjoy this hike. If you're not, you'll love it. Panther Creek Trail, as you might guess, follows the shore of Panther Creek. This is the second Panther Creek (and second Panther Creek Falls) in this book. The other one is in the Cohuttas (see p. 70). Although panthers left the area long ago, they were once common in the north Georgia mountains, and people tended to name creeks after them. So you won't see any big cats, but you *will* see four pretty waterfalls, one of which is spectacular.

Hiking along Panther Creek Trail is quite enjoyable—aside from the disturbing underpass crossing below the noisy four-lane within the first half-mile. Once beyond that, everything is delightful. The trail follows the creek almost the entire way. Early on you'll be high above it. In fact, to get down to the first falls, you'll need to take a side trail which is actually part of an older abandoned route, then scramble down to the creekside. Let the sound of the crashing waterfall lead you to the falls. The other waterfalls are easily viewed from the trail.

First Falls on Panther Creek
Class: Tiered/slide Height: 35 ft Rating: Good

Upon reaching Panther Creek Falls, you're in for a real treat. The trail leads you out onto some giant boulders right at the very top of the waterfall. You get a commanding view of both the falls and the large plunge pool at its base. If there is anyone down there, they'll look pretty small. The trail continues on down to the bottom where you can take a swim or eat your lunch before making the return hike to your car.

So what does a fear of heights have to do with this hike? Panther Creek carves its way through some very rugged terrain. On several occasions steep bluffs nearly block passage of the trail. Evidently the trail builders won out, but just barely. As you'll see, in places the trail barely clings to the sides of the bluffs. These spots require you to negotiate a 2-foot-wide tread with a rock cliff pressing against one shoulder and a cliff under your feet, with nothing between you and the creek far below except (sometimes) a thin hand cable and (always) a lot of thin air. It can take your breath away.

Second Falls on Panther Creek
Class: Slide Height: 15 ft Rating: Fair

Panther Creek Trail (cont.)

Getting to the Trailhead

From Tallulah Gorge State Park, go south on US 441 for 2.6 miles and turn right on Old 441 South. Drive 1.5 miles to the trailhead.

GPS Coordinates
N 34° 41.92' W 83° 25.19'

Hiking Directions

Begin Walk across the road and onto Panther Creek Trail where you'll soon pass underneath the four-lane.

Mile 0.9 Pass beneath an overhanging cave-like rock. Just beyond, you'll hear the first waterfall down to the right, a 15-foot, two-tiered drop onto a 75-yard-long, 20-foot-high waterslide, down off the right fork. After viewing the falls, come back and take the left fork.

Mile 2.6 Reach a bluff overlooking the second waterfall, a 15-foot waterslide.

Mile 3.7 After hiking along several stretches of trail where the path barely clings to the mountainside high above the creek,

you'll come to a very high bluff overlooking Panther Creek Falls. It's a long way to the bottom. Up here you can view the top falls, a 35-foot tiered drop ending in a sluice. Follow the trail to the bottom.

Mile 3.9 Reach the bottom of Panther Creek Falls. This is a seriously big waterfall with a huge plunge pool. It's a great place to take a swim or eat lunch. From here, return the way you came.

Mile 7.8 Finish.

TOP FALLS JUST ABOVE PANTHER CREEK FALLS
Class: Tier/Sluice Height: 35 ft Rating: Good

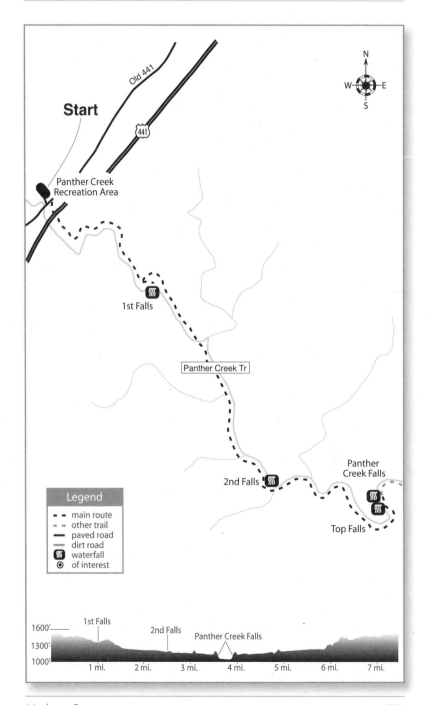

Start

Old 441

441

Panther Creek
Recreation Area

1st Falls

Panther Creek Tr

2nd Falls

Panther
Creek Falls

Top Falls

Legend
- - main route
- - other trail
— paved road
— dirt road
▨ waterfall
◉ of interest

N
W   E
S

1600'
1300'
1000'

1st Falls

2nd Falls

Panther Creek Falls

1 mi.   2 mi.   3 mi.   4 mi.   5 mi.   6 mi.   7 mi.

Sourwood Trail

Hike Distance:	3.9 miles
Type of Hike:	Loop
Number of Falls:	2
Hiking Time:	Half day
Dry Feet:	Yes
Start Elevation:	1,066 ft
Total Ascent:	541 ft
Land Manager:	USFS
Fee:	None

NANCYTOWN FALLS
Class: Tiered Height: 25 ft Rating: Fair

This hike is just barely in the mountains, therefore both the trail and the waterfalls have a somewhat different character than those found higher up in the hills. It's nonetheless an enjoyable hike—not too strenuous, and a good choice should winter weather make mountain travel difficult or less desirable.

The absence of high mountains in the area is noticeable almost immediately. Drive along US 441 heading north from Cornelia, and you can see them in the distance, standing up against the horizon like a grayish-blue wall poking up through the haze. Your immediate surroundings are mere hills in comparison.

Once on the trail, the differences may be less obvious. Notice the soil where the trail has eroded. In the mountains it would be rocky and dark; here it is red clay. There is still plenty of mountain laurel and rhododendron, but look at the trees. Much of this forest is southern pine, and there tends to be much more underbrush. Once you get out to the waterfalls, it even feels different. You get the sense that these falls don't quite fit the terrain, and you want to say, "What are you fellows doing here? This isn't the place for a 25-foot waterfall." Whether they seem to fit or not, they are here, and they certainly add to the enjoyment of hiking this loop.

Sourwood Trail gets its name from the sourwood tree. Interestingly, there aren't many sourwoods along this trail; look closely, and you'll see only a few. This tree tends to grow well in disturbed areas, reaches heights of 40 or 50 feet, and frequently has a diameter of 6 to 10 inches. It's one of the last trees to bloom in June and one of the first to turn a bright red in October, before dropping its leaves altogether. When oxen were still used to pull a plow, farmers would use a section of a sourwood log as a yoke since the tree almost always had a bend in it that suited that purpose. Sourwood was also used to make sled runners.

Possibly the most notable product of a sourwood tree is the honey produced from its nectar. Sourwood honey is anything but sour. In fact, it is regionally famous and sought after by locals and visitors alike. Very light in color to the point of being nearly clear, its flavor is out-of-this-world good. Like its color, its taste is light and sweet with a slight zing to it. On at least one occasion, sourwood honey produced in north Georgia has placed first in international competition. Look for it at roadside stands and farmers' markets in mid- to late summer.

Following Sourwood Trail is easy. It's well marked with green blazes and frequently used. You'll pass through stands of pine as well as forests of mixed hardwoods. Once down by Nancytown Creek, the woods more closely resemble those in the mountains. You'll see two waterfalls and cross what many years ago was a beaver pond, now filled in and providing a rich habitat for new plants.

LOWER FALLS ON NANCYTOWN CREEK
Class: Tiered Height: 10 ft Rating: Nice

Sourwood Trail (cont.)

Getting to the Trailhead

From US 441 Bus. in Cornelia, take Dicks Hill Parkway north 2.0 miles and turn right on Lake Russell Road. Drive another 1.9 miles down the hill, then turn left to follow the signs for the group camping area. Park at the gate.

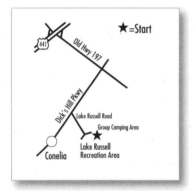

GPS Coordinates
N 34° 29.95' W 83° 29.07'

Hiking Directions

Begin Walk around the gate and down the road toward the group camping area.

Mile 0.4 Just before the bridge, turn left on Sourwood Trail (#155).

Mile 1.3 Cross Nancytown Road. In another half-mile or so you'll cross over a ridge and begin to hear the falls up ahead.

Mile 1.8 Turn left on the spur trail to Nancytown Falls.

Mile 1.9 Reach Nancytown Falls, a 25-foot-high broken horsetail fan surrounded by mountain laurel and Carolina rhododendron. After viewing the falls, retrace your steps on the spur trail and then continue on around the loop.

Mile 2.2 Pass through the remnants of an old beaver pond, now filled in. The trail follows alongside Nancytown Creek, passing several small shoals and falls.

Mile 2.9 Turn right on FS 92. Immediately on your right are the lower falls on Nancytown Creek, a 10-foot, double-tiered drop with a shallow plunge pool at the bottom.

Mile 3.3 Turn left on FS 591.

Mile 3.5 Go around the gate, over the bridge, and bear left on the paved road. This completes the loop. To return to the trailhead, continue on the paved road.

Mile 3.9 Finish.

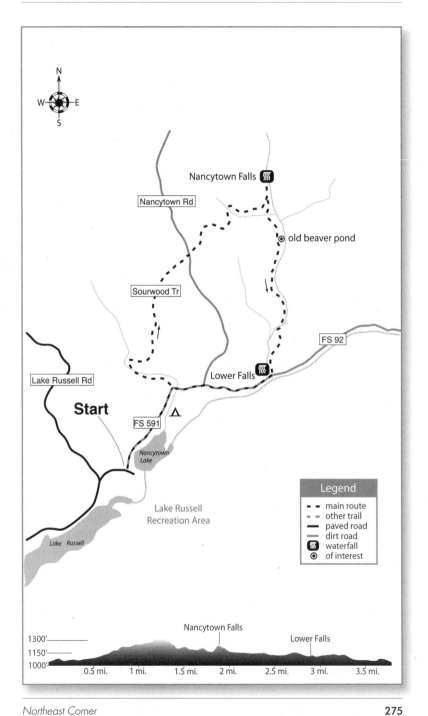

N
W—E
S

Nancytown Falls ▓

Nancytown Rd

● old beaver pond

Sourwood Tr

FS 92

Lake Russell Rd

Start

Lower Falls ▓

△

FS 591

Nancytown Lake

Lake Russell Recreation Area

Lake Russell

Legend
- - main route
- - other trail
—— paved road
—— dirt road
▓ waterfall
◉ of interest

1300'———
1150'———
1000'———

Nancytown Falls

Lower Falls

0.5 mi.   1 mi.   1.5 mi.   2 mi.   2.5 mi.   3 mi.   3.5 mi.

Appendices

AMICALOLA FALLS

Appendix A—Resources Contact Information

Chattahoochee National Forest (USFS)

Forest Supervisor's Office
Chattahoochee–Oconee National Forests
1755 Cleveland Highway
Gainesville, GA 30501
770-297-3000
fs.usda.gov/conf

Armuchee–Cohutta Ranger District
3941 Highway 76
Chatsworth, GA 30705
706-695-6736

Brasstown Ranger District
1881 Highway 515, PO Box 9
Blairsville, GA 30514
706-745-6928

Chattooga Ranger District
200 Highway 197 N, PO Box 1960
Clarkesville, GA 30523
706-754-6221

Tallulah Ranger District
809 Highway 441 South
Clayton, GA 30525
706-782-3320

Toccoa Ranger District
6050 Appalachian Highway
Blue Ridge, GA 30513
706-632-3031

Georgia Department of Natural Resources

Georgia State Parks
1352 Floyd Tower East
2 Martin Luther King Drive
Atlanta, GA 30334
800-864-7275
GeorgiaStateParks.org

Amicalola Falls State Park
418 Amicalola Falls State Park Road
Dawsonville, GA 30534
706-265-4703
GeorgiaStateParks.org

Cloudland Canyon State Park
122 Cloudland Canyon State Park Road
Rising Fawn, GA 30738
706-657-4050
GeorgiaStateParks.org

Fort Mountain State Park
181 Fort Mountain Park Road
Chatsworth, GA 30705
706-422-1932
GeorgiaStateParks.org

Tallulah Gorge State Park
PO Box 248
Tallulah Falls, GA 30573
706-754-7970
GeorgiaStateParks.org

Georgia Department of Natural Resources–Wildlife Resources

Wildlife Resources Division State Headquarters
2070 US Highway 278 SE
Social Circle, GA 30025
770-918-6400
gohuntgeorgia.com

Northwest Region Office (Crockford-Pigeon Mountain WMA)
2592 Floyd Springs Road
Armuchee, GA 30105
706-295-6041

Northeast Region Office (Dawson Forest Wildcat & Amicalola Tract)
2150 Dawsonville Highway
Gainesville, GA 30501
770-535-5700

Land Trusts

Lula Lake Land Trust (LLLT)
PO Box 395
Lookout Mountain, TN 37350
lulalake.org

National Park Service

Chickamauga and Chattanooga National Military Park
PO Box 2128
Fort Oglethorpe, GA 30742
706-866-9241
nps.gov/chch

Appendix B—Suggested Itineraries

Generally speaking, you'll be hard pressed to tackle more than one of the hikes listed in this book in a day. However, it does include some shorter hikes which can be combined or done in conjunction with another when they are close enough. Those are listed below by region. For those who like a challenge, I've also listed some ideas for knocking off a couple of longer hikes—and seeing all the waterfalls!—in one day.

Northwest Corner

Lula Lake Land Trust Loop (p. 34) and Glen Falls Trail (p. 38)
The trailheads for these two hikes are only about five miles apart. If you're coming from Chattanooga, hike to Glen Falls first. If you're coming from the south, go to Lula Lake first, then drive over and hike to Glen Falls. After that, you can catch a meal at one of the eclectic selection of restaurants at the bottom of Lookout Mountain, only moments away.

Cohutta Mountains

Shadow Falls (p. 82) and Mountaintown Creek Trail (p. 78)
The hike to Shadow Falls is pretty short, but the drive to get there is really long. To make it worth your while, you'll want to add another hike. Mountaintown Creek Trail is the closest, only two miles up the road.

Mill Creek Falls (p. 66) and Panther Creek Falls (p. 70)
You would not want to do both of these hikes in the same day, but consider this variation. The hike out to Panther Creek Falls is quite long, and so is the drive to the trailhead. Why not get a jump-start on the day by camping the night before at Hickey Gap, a free Forest Service campground which is the trailhead for the hike to the falls on Mill Creek? It's only a 2.5-mile drive from Hickey Gap to the trailhead for the Panther Creek Falls hike. You can make the short hike out to see the falls on Mill Creek in the evening after you set up your tent and have dinner.

Western Blue Ridge

Three Forks West (p. 108)–Little Rock Creek Falls (p. 112)–Sea Creek Falls (p. 116) Tour

In this scenario, you'll get to drive a nice loop on Forest Service roads up onto some of the highest dirt roads in Georgia, do three short hikes, and pick up a couple of bonus falls as well—definitely a full day's outing. Start by heading up to Three Forks on FS 58, stopping off at Noontootla Falls along the way. After the Three Forks hike, circle around the high ridges above the Appalachian Trail on FS 42 and FS 69. Stop off at Rock Creek Lake for a late picnic lunch and get a look at Rock Creek Falls. After that, continue down to the short hike at Little Rock Creek, then skip over via GA 60 to end the day with the easy hike to Sea Creek Falls.

The Three Sisters Roundup: Amicalola (p. 134), Cochrans (p. 130), and Bearden (p. 126) Falls

An early start is essential if you want to see all three of these "sisters" in one day—and it will be one *full* day! Each one falls off the same escarpment, and they're only a few miles apart as the crow flies, but when the day is done, you'll have hiked 10.6 miles. Do Amicalola first. You'll see fewer people out early in the morning, and it's nice not to climb all those steps at the end of the day. Then drive down the road to Cochrans and have a look at it; that will be your longest hike. Finally, end the day with a walk up to Bearden.

Eastern Blue Ridge

Little Ridge Creek Falls (p. 190) and Cowrock Creek Falls (p. 194)

Both these hikes are in the Boggs Creek Recreation Area, and the trailheads are only 0.3 mile apart. Do them both, and you'll have hiked three miles and seen six waterfalls.

Blood Mountain Creek Falls (p. 196) and Crow Mountain Creek Falls (p. 200)

These two hikes are in a waterfall-rich area off the same Forest Service road, FS 34. Not only will you see the two falls while you're hiking, you'll see four bonus falls on the way there. In all, you'll walk about four miles.

Northeast Corner

Angel Falls Trail (p. 252), Minnehaha Falls Trail (p. 256), Bad Branch Falls (p. 258), and Crow Creek Falls (p. 260)

This might seem like a lot to bite off, but all these hikes are fairly close to each other, and by the end of the trip you'll have hiked just 3.8 miles and seen seven waterfalls. Start with Crow Creek and work your way back to Angel Falls—that way, if you came from anywhere along US 441, you'll be closer to home at the end of the day.

Appendix C—Highest Waterfalls

Different guidebooks, the web, and other sources make all kinds of claims as to which are the highest waterfalls in any given region of the world. This seems especially prevalent in the eastern U.S. For instance, Georgia, Tennessee, North Carolina, and Virginia all claim to have the highest waterfall east of the Mississippi. Who's right? It's hard to say—and it depends on so many variables. What constitutes a single waterfall? Where's the absolute top? Where's the absolute bottom? Just when you think you've got a good list going, someone will point out some tiny, obscure creek that plunges off a 500-foot cliff, like the ones falling into Tallulah Gorge in Georgia or the Great Bend Gorge of the Genesee River in New York. In case you're interested in joining the debate, here's a list of high waterfalls to get you started. See if you can find any higher—or, reasons to dispute the heights of these.

Highest Waterfall in the World

Angel Falls	3,281 ft	Venezuela

Highest Waterfall in the United States

Yosemite Falls	2,425 ft	California

10 Highest Waterfalls East of the Mississippi

Crabtree Falls	1,200 ft	Virginia
Glassmine Falls	800 ft	North Carolina
Amicalola Falls	729 ft	Georgia
Cochrans Falls	600 ft	Georgia
Caledonia Cascade	600 ft	Georgia
Corbin Creek Falls	600 ft	North Carolina
Panther Creek Falls (Cohuttas)	450 ft	Georgia
Upper Whitewater Falls	411 ft	North Carolina
Hickory Nut Falls	404 ft	North Carolina
Raven Cliff Falls	400 ft	South Carolina

Appendix D—Index of Waterfall Photos

thru-hikers 109, 135
Tobacco Pouch Trail 144–145
Trahlyta Falls 184
Turkey Trail 36–37

U

U.S. Army Ranger Training
    118–119

W

Warwoman Dell 210, 228–231
    Falls 229
West Brow Trail 44–45
White Twister Trail 249–250
Whitewater
    Falls (NC) 284
    kayaking 66
    rafting 232–233
Wildcat Creek
    Trail (Dawson Forest Wildcat
    Tract) 102, 144–149
    waterfalls (near
    Lake Burton) 245
Wildcat Tract 102, 142, 144,
    146
wilderness (defined) 57
Wilks Creek Waterfalls 160
Windy Ridge Trail 144

Y

York Creek Falls 166
Yosemite Falls (CA) 284

TRAIL NOTES

Milestone Press

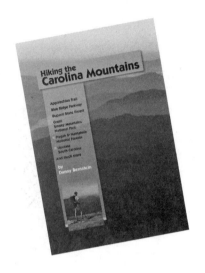

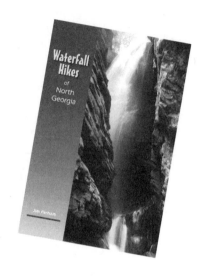

Hiking

- *Hiking the Carolina Mountains* by Danny Bernstein

- *Hiking North Carolina's Blue Ridge Mountains* by Danny Bernstein

- *Day Hiking the North Georgia Mountains* by Jim Parham

- *Waterfalls Hikes of Upstate South Carolina* by Thomas E. King

- *Waterfalls Hikes of North Georgia* by Jim Parham

- *Hiking Atlanta's Hidden Forests: Intown & Out* by Jonah McDonald

- *Backpacking Overnights: North Carolina Mountains South Carolina Upstate* by Jim Parham

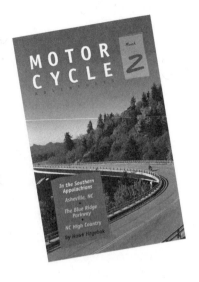

Motorcycle Adventure Series
by Hawk Hagebak

- *1–Southern Appalachians:
  North GA, East TN,
  Western NC*

- *2–Southern Appalachians:
  Asheville NC,
  Blue Ridge Parkway,
  NC High Country*

- *3–Central Appalachians:
  Virginia's Blue Ridge,
  Shenandoah Valley,
  West Virginia Highlands*

**Off the Beaten Track
Mountain Bike Guide Series**
by Jim Parham

- *Vol. 1: WNC–Smokies*
- *Vol. 2: WNC–Pisgah*
- *Vol. 3: N. Georgia*
- *Vol. 4: E. Tennessee*
- *Vol. 5: N. Virginia*

Milestone Press

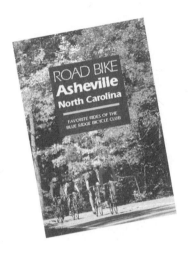

Road Bike Guide Series

- *Road Bike Asheville, NC: Favorite Rides of the Blue Ridge Bicycle Club* by The Blue Ridge Bicycle Club

- *Road Bike North Georgia: 25 Great Rides in the Mountains and Valleys of North Georgia* by Jim Parham

- *Road Bike the Smokies* by Jim Parham

Family Adventure

- *Natural Adventures in the Mountains of North Georgia* by Mary Ellen Hammond & Jim Parham

- *Family Hikes in Upstate South Carolina* by Scott Lynch

Rockhounding

- *A Rockhounding Guide
  to North Carolina's Blue
  Ridge Mountains*
  by Michael Streeter

Can't find the Milestone Press book you want at a bookseller near you?
Don't despair—you can order it directly from us. Call us at
828-488-6601 or shop online at www.milestonepress.com.

Great Hikes
of the Southern Appalachians

Put the hikes from this book on your phone.

iPhone or Android

Taking a hike doesn't get much easier! With hundreds of routes to choose from in Western North Carolina, Upstate South Carolina, North Georgia, and metro Atlanta, this mobile app helps you search and select a hike, get to the trailhead, and find your way on the trail. All hikes are adapted from Milestone Press's best guidebooks, so you know they're created by expert hikers and tested by countless users. Watch for updates as more routes are added to the list! Once you've purchased and installed the GPS-enabled hikes on your phone, all your trail information is fully functional, with no wi-fi or data connection required.

All your favorite hikes from this and other Milestone Press guidebooks are now accessible on your smart phone.

- Hundreds of hikes to choose from in the mountains of North and South Carolina and Georgia, as well as the Atlanta metro area

- GPS-enabled so you always know precisely where you are on the trail and en route to the trailhead

- Look for **Great Hikes of the Southern Appalachians** at the Apple App or Google Play store.

- Downloading the app is easy. Just scan the QR code with your iPhone or android for direct access to **Great Hikes**.

An App for iPhone or Android